"An Evoluti … t as Seen Through Mosaic Art,"

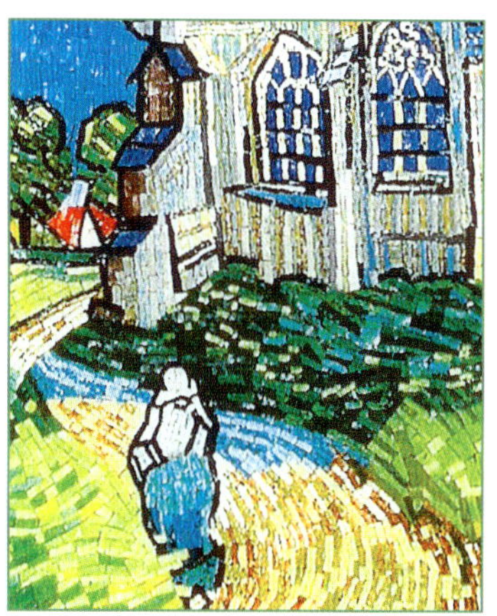

A PRESENTATION OF

The Vatican Mosaic Studio and the Archdiocese of New Orleans' Catholic Cultural Heritage Center

OLD URSULINE CONVENT
JANUARY – JUNE 2007

I am particularly pleased that the Archdiocese of New Orleans will host so graciously this Exhibition of mosaic masterpieces produced by the Vatican Mosaic Studio, some of which have been executed for the first time specifically for this important event. I would like this Exhibition to communicate to all the faithful of the Archdiocese, as well as all the inhabitants of New Orleans, the warm spiritual embrace of brotherhood that extends from the Patriarchal Basilica of St. Peter as the fundamental mortar onto which each culture of faith is impressed as a mosaic tessera within the consciousness of the Universal Church.

One of the essential qualities for which mosaic craftsmanship has been valued and appreciated throughout the centuries is its potential luminous and translucent character as well as the durability of the materials employed. This is the major reason why it was chosen to decorate the Basilica as it stands today and the Constantinian structure that preceded it which rose to mark the stone upon which the Universal Church was to be built, the tomb of the Apostle Peter. The employment of this technique offers then a visible sign of the ongoing concern of the Church throughout the centuries to look after and support the preservation, rebuilding, renovation of built heritage as a necessary treasure of human development.

Light is essential in order to see and perceive creation, others, and ourselves. Light is essential to life. Our faith should be a continuous bright source of light accompanying every day of our lives, even and especially when tragic events occur. Every day lived in faith should become the rock of our existence and our ticket of participation in God's promised eternal life.

The mosaic works on display should impart a ray of this light to all who admire them, reminding us of the principal calling of Christian art to serve as a spiritual quenching force, to communicate a salvific message of hope and life, to educate towards brotherhood and peace. In this demanding rebuilding phase of urban planning, may the citizens of New Orleans find this Exhibition a source of encouragement and consolation.

I wish to thank the Archdiocese of New Orleans, particularly Archbishop Alfred Hughes for his fraternal support and friendship and the Auxiliary Bishops of the Archdiocese who have come to visit the Vatican Mosaic Studio to show their appreciation; Monsignor Crosby Kern, Rector of the St. Louis Cathedral of New Orleans, for his inspiring, enthusiastic and energetic efforts in making this possible; Dr. Charles Nolan, all the Archdiocesan and Cathedral staff members for their hospitality and caring concern when I and my staff had the wonderful chance to come and begin planning the Exhibition. I would like to thank everyone who has offered their precious financial support and time in the realization of this extraordinary event, especially the illustrious Patrons of the Cultural Center, representatives of governmental agencies, and scholars from the local museum communities.

I hope that this exhibition and the activities that are planned around it, especially the educational programs, may represent for the entire community of New Orleans, a moment of deep spiritual and cultural enrichment, an occasion to feel a little closer to the hearts of those here at the Fabbrica and working for the Basilica who with sentiments of gratitude and affection remember each one of you in their prayers.

Francesco Card. Marchisano

Francesco Cardinal Marchisano
Archpriest
Patriarchal Basilica of Saint Peter

It is my privilege to welcome you to the first extensive exhibition of the Vatican Mosaic Studio to be held outside of Rome. The Archdiocese of New Orleans considers it a great honor to host this remarkable exhibition of "An Evolution of the Human Spirit as Seen Through Mosaic Art" created in the Vatican Mosaic Studio. It is my particular pleasure to also welcome you to the newly-opened Old Ursuline Convent, one of our many buildings that suffered major damage from Hurricane Katrina and its aftermath. This exhibition and the reopening of the convent mark another milestone in the post-Katrina recovery of the archdiocese and the wider community.

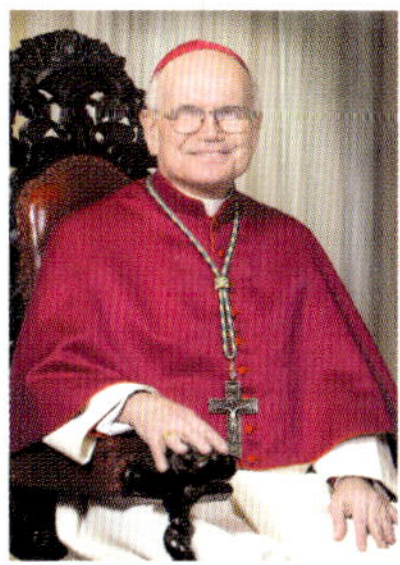

I wish to first acknowledge and thank His Eminence, Francesco Cardinal Marchisano. His leadership as the founding president of the Pontifical Commission for the Cultural Heritage of the Church has provided both the inspiration and direction for our new Cultural Heritage Center. As the Archpriest of St. Peter's Basilica in Rome and the former president of the basilica's Fabbrica, he has both encouraged and facilitated this rare exhibition. Archbishop Angelo Comastri, the new president of the Fabbrica of St. Peter's Basilica, has graciously endorsed and supported the plan which Cardinal Marchisano initiated.

I am deeply grateful to Dr. Cristina Carlo-Stella, the basilica's chief-of-staff, for her significant role in preparing the exhibition and compiling this accompanying catalogue. Dr. Paolo DiBuono, director of the Vatican Mosaic Studio, worked generously and effectively with the center's staff to plan and implement the exhibition. In addition, he has generously offered to provide a small group of youth of our area with a unique opportunity for hands-on learning about the art of mosaic making.

Msgr. Crosby W. Kern, Rector of St. Louis Cathedral, has exercised dynamic leadership in establishing our new Catholic Cultural Heritage Center which officially opened on October 1, 2004. He and his staff have successfully accepted the extraordinary responsibility and honor of hosting this exhibition, particularly in the difficult months following Hurricane Katrina.

This exhibition would never have happened without the enthusiastic support of the Center's Board of Directors under the leadership of Barbara Turner Windhorst and many volunteers who have worked to make this exhibit possible. Mrs. Phyllis Taylor has provided pivotal leadership as Chair for the exhibition. Both have helped us to realize the collaboration and support of the wider New Orleans community.

It is my pleasure to extend a special invitation to each of you to enjoy and benefit from this exhibition of "An Evolution of the Human Spirit as Seen Through Mosaic Art" in our Catholic Cultural Heritage Center.

Most Reverend Alfred C. Hughes
Archbishop of New Orleans
January 26, 2007

ART SPEAKS TO MEN'S HEARTS

On December 25th, 1886, Paul Claudel entered as an atheist inside the Cathedral of Notre-Dame in Paris and came out singing the Magnificat with the exuberant joy of a boy who had just found his father and mother.

He himself recalls: "This is how an unhappy young man went to see Notre-Dame in Paris on December 25th to assist the Christmas celebration. I had just begun writing and I had the impression that in Catholic ceremonies, considered to be superior in their amateurship, I would have found some inspiration to write about a decadent experience. With this in mind, as I elbowed my way through the crowd, I assisted the solemn Mass with little interest. Then, since I had nothing better to do, I returned in the afternoon to assist the vespers ceremony.

The choir boys, dressed in white, the students of the minor seminary of St. Nicolas du Chardonnet were singing what I understood later to be the Magnificat. I remained standing among the crowd of faithful near the second pilaster at the entrance of the choir, to the right near the sacristy.

In that precise moment a strange event took place, the event that was to dominate my entire life. In an instant my heart was touched and I believed.

I believed with a force and conviction so great and powerful, with such an uplifting sense of my entire being, with a certainty that did not leave any space for doubt. After that no reasoning, no circumstance of my agitated life could shake my faith nor touch it.

Suddenly I had the lacerating sentiment of innocence, of the eternal infancy of God: a fleeting reaction! As I try to remember back the moments that followed this extraordinary instant, as I do often, I can identify the following thoughts as flashbacks, as one single means used by divine Providence to reach and finally open the heart of a poor desperate individual: how happy are those who believe! Was it true? Was it really true? God exists, He is here. He is someone, a personal Being as me! He loves me, He calls me. Tears and sobbing had emerged while emotion had increased as I heard the tender melody of Adeste fideles."

The experience of Paul Claudel confirms to us that what is truly beautiful is surely also good: beauty and goodness, in fact, are two sides of God's mystery. It is clear, then, that the encounter with beauty (the beauty of singing, the beauty of a painting, the beauty of a mosaic, the beauty of a cathedral...) makes man closer to God. It allows, if man's heart is open humbly to this experience, a pleasant encounter with the Light, and thus, with joy, which is the absolute prerogative of God.

I wish that this Exhibition of mosaics produced by the Vatican Mosaic Studio of the Fabbrica of St. Peter in the Vatican, may bring a ray of light to the city of New Orleans, so that visitors may perceive the enchanting Beauty of God.

+ Angelo Comastri
President, Fabbrica San Pietro
Vicar General of the Holy Father for
Vatican City State

Table of Contents

FORWORD:

MESSAGE FROM THE DIRECTOR

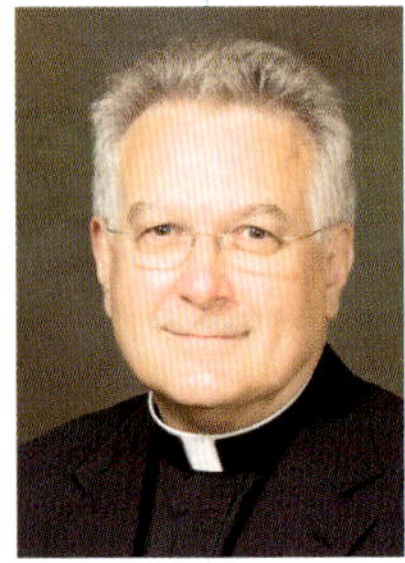

Wisdom, beauty, truth, knowledge, love - these are concepts that man has always sought in his quest to know God. Throughout recorded history, these concepts have been expressed in literature, art, and music. Man has used his senses to try to explain the abstract. The haunting vision of a sunset or a lilting melody of the wind, the explanation of the physical nature of creation, all have been a part of the human expression. Man has portrayed these concepts in various ways, one of which is mosaic art.

The earliest examples of mosaic art date from the time of the Babylonians, about six centuries before Christ. It is the first known attempt of man to express himself in colored tiles arranged in patterns to decorate palaces and temples. This was the first known attempt to enhance the human spirit in this art form. From that time up to the present new techniques and materials have contributed to mosaic art. The Greeks, Romans, and every age since have produced mosaics. The Vatican grottos and some catacombs show examples of ancient religious mosaics, both pagan and Christian. Many of these are used in church decoration today.

With the construction of the new St. Peter's Basilica in the sixteenth century, a need arose for a studio that would decorate the new building. Thus was founded the Vatican Mosaic Studio. The Studio has not only been responsible for the decoration of the Basilica with religious art, but has also been responsible for the continued restoration of those works. As time has passed, the Studio, developing new techniques, has reproduced ancient works, copies from the masters, and new creations in mosaics. These works can be seen in St. Peter's and in the Studio today.

For the first time since the 16th century, the Vatican Mosaic Studio and the Catholic Cultural Center of the Archdiocese of New Orleans are proud to present this first comprehensive exhibition of mosaic art outside of the Vatican. We hope to show the art form and to show the works produced by the Studio. This exhibition will tell the story of the production and restoration of mosaics. It will tell the story of an evolution of the human spirit as seen through mosaic art. It will help us understand those concepts of beauty, truth, wisdom, and love; it will help us in our quest to know God.

Rev. Msgr. Crosby W. Kern
Director

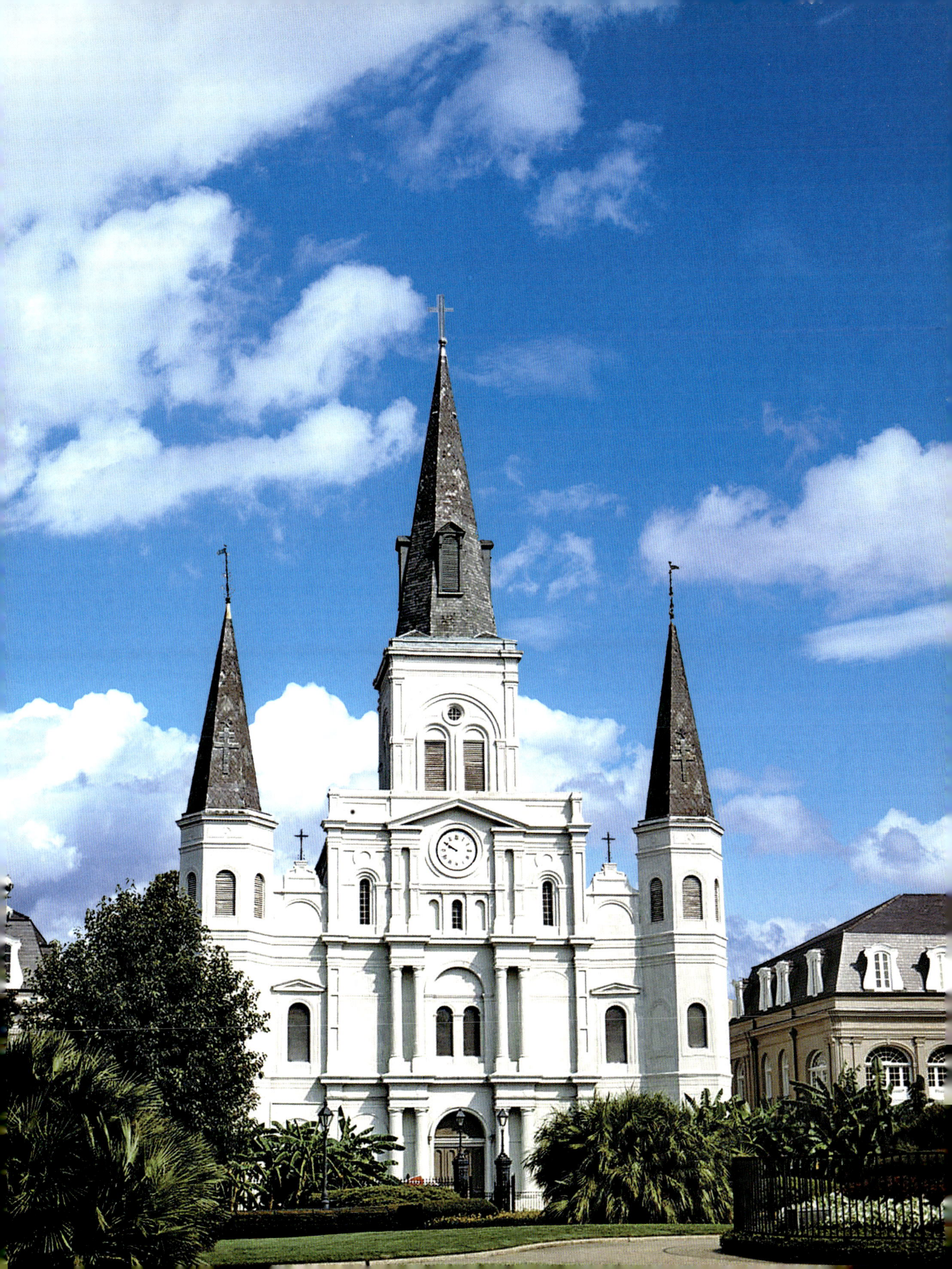

Preface

By Dr. Cristina Carlo-Stella, FSP, Chief-of-Staff

We are honored and delighted that this splendid Archdiocesan Cultural Center, which represents an eloquent landmark not only for local, regional and national history and social history but also for the ecclesial history of this great nation, has decided to host a very special exhibition of mosaic masterpieces produced by the Vatican Mosaic Studio. This is not the first time that works by the Studio have arrived in this country.

Archival evidence tells us that about 145 years ago (in 1860) one of our first mosaic masterpieces to cross the ocean reached this nation at Bostonian shores. It was commissioned by a private individual and executed by one of the best mosaic artists of the Vatican Studio - Barbieri. It was to announce a patronage tradition from this country that has steadily increased throughout these years and continues strong to this day. At the time of that early commission, the Vatican Mosaic Studio had just begun functioning as a permanent structured entity within the Fabbrica (1845), after a thirty year period of French Imperial rule. Thirty years had also just passed (in 1831) since the closing of a branch of the Studio in Paris, founded back in 1798 and headed by the well-known Vatican mosaicist Belloni.

Clearly it was a period of intense market expansion for the Vatican Studio which by 1850 had also established a branch in St. Petersburg. It is curious to note that the same work that received the commission by our Bostonian patron was the one that enkindled the interest of Tsar Nicholas I some years before leading to his support for the opening of the St. Petersburg branch.

This policy of market expansionism was facilitated not only through the contacts established under the French Imperial rule of Rome but certainly also by the fact that by the beginning of the 19th century Vatican Studio mosaic artists had just completed a major Herculean feat for the Basilica of St. Peter: the transcription in mosaic technique of all the pictorial surfaces, particularly the *pale d'altare* or altar pieces of the major chapels, covering an area of about 10,000 square meters, in order to assure a better preservation of these surfaces for posterity. The task had begun on an experimental level in 1627 for the vault and cupola of the Gregorian Chapel. The success of this tremendous undertaking depended on two major achievements:

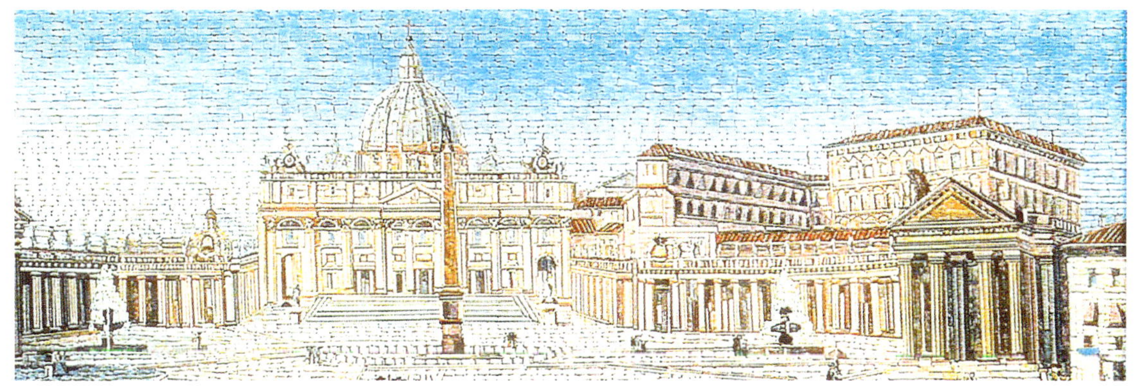

Detail of St. Peter's Square*. Reproduction from a painting of anonymous author, 19th century A.D.*

the development of innovative mosaic techniques devised by the Studio; as well as an underlying concern for recovering and reviving the artistic tradition of the Early Church community which had as its fundamental intrinsic aim a didactic function for catechesis - a tradition that chose the mosaic medium as one of its most eloquent expressions. The new St. Peter's, designed by artistic geniuses such as Bramante, Michelangelo, Maderno and Bernini, was to symbolize this exciting and inspiring moment of renewal for ecclesiology, for ecclesial artistic heritage and for humantistic creativity in general.

By the time the Boston commission was successfully delivered, the Vatican Mosaic Studio had pretty much prefigured its two major tasks: on the one hand the supervision/preservation/restoration of mosaic surfaces inside the Basilica; and the production of masterpieces for private commissions. In 1795 the Studio had been authorized to execute not only religious works but also works with secular subject matter, which of course opened up market possibilities.

Two hundred and ten years have gone by since that decision was taken which allowed for that early commission to reach America. Now this exhibition in New Orleans intends to re-address the challenge behind one of the two achievements that allowed the successful completion of the decorative program of new St. Peter's, that is, to re-propose the enhancement of artistic creation as a vehicle for spiritual enrichment. It is quite fitting that this theme be re-proposed to today's society at a most significant time in the history of this Basilica as it coincides with the celebration of the Quinquennial anniversary of its foundation[1]. It is a message that should reach out and touch every individual, establish a personal dialogue, open up mind and soul to the "good news" of the divine presence in creation and the potential of artistic creativity as a medium to capture that presence!

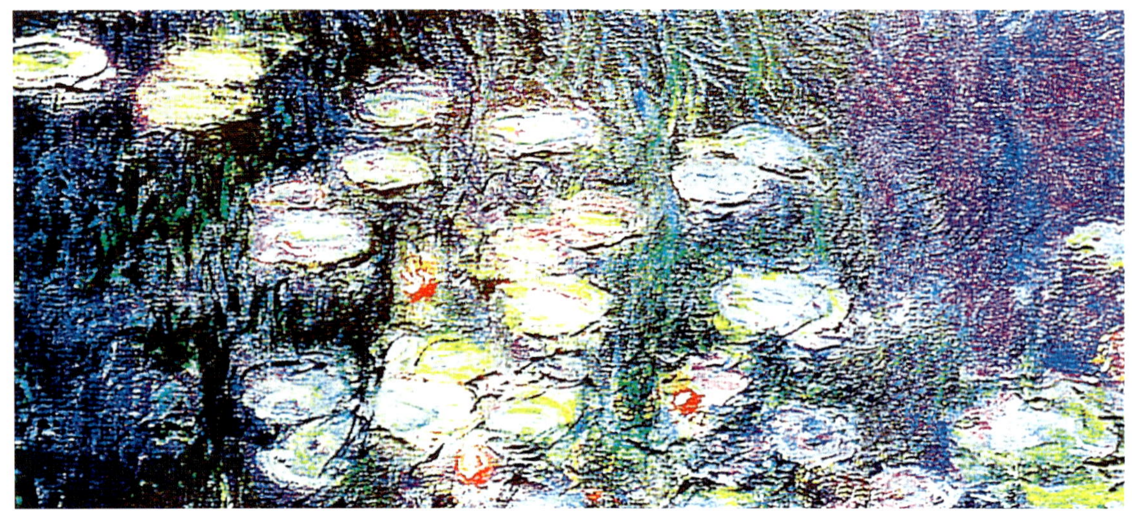

Detail of W*ATER* L*ILIES*. *Reproduction of the painting by Claude Monet, mid-19th century*

More than thirty works, of which twenty have never been exhibited before and ten have been produced for the first time by the Vatican Mosaic Studio, have been carefully selected to present a comprehensive corpus that spans a variety of subjects, both religious and secular, and reflect the stylistic evolution of pictorial art through the ages, including well-known masterpieces from the Renaissance period, up until the modern as well as contemporary periods with works inspired from famous canvases by Monet, Van Gogh, Chagall and Rouault. Although the works exhibited are thus modeled after these chef-d'œuvres, each work should be considered unique as the transposition process into a new technique with its own specific qualities pertaining to the particular medium applied, necessarily brings about a new perspective and induces us to look at the model subject under a different light, that can only enrich its appreciation and value.

Indeed, mosaic technique can present a truly "cosmic" perspective of the creative process as it encompasses necessarily both an analytical and synthetic approach, as well as proposes a means through which one can observe how the materiality of form can interrelate and interact with sensual perception, and thus reveal the complexity of the visual process perhaps offering new insights into color theory and the phenomenon of illusionism. We can even say that the historical development of this technique has progressed alongside this scientific-empirical investigation of the art of perception. It has often resulted in a curious and inspiring dialogue between naturalistic and abstract forms that projected through a kaleidoscopic fusion of reflected and refracted lights, dissolve architectural barriers and create in the beholder an experience of marvel and awe, a transcendental experience of that melodic or symphonic harmony and beauty that can be communicated by artistic creation.

We hope that this exhibition in New Orleans may also represent an opportunity to address two other major challenges. The first concerns the actual survival of mosaic craftsmanship. In many parts of the world where this medium had flourished for centuries, not only as centers of production but also as educational centers, interest and resources are quickly dying out. What emerges as worrying is not only a lack of economic possibilities needed to keep these centers going, but more so a hiatus in the handing down process of practical knowledge between generations of craftsmen as young generations, even within families of mosaic artists, seem to have lost interest. If they do develop an interest there are only a few professional centers that can assure adequate quality training according to serious educational standards and provide that institutional recognition that can turn this interest into a thriving profession able to survive and meet the requests of our present-day marketing mentality.

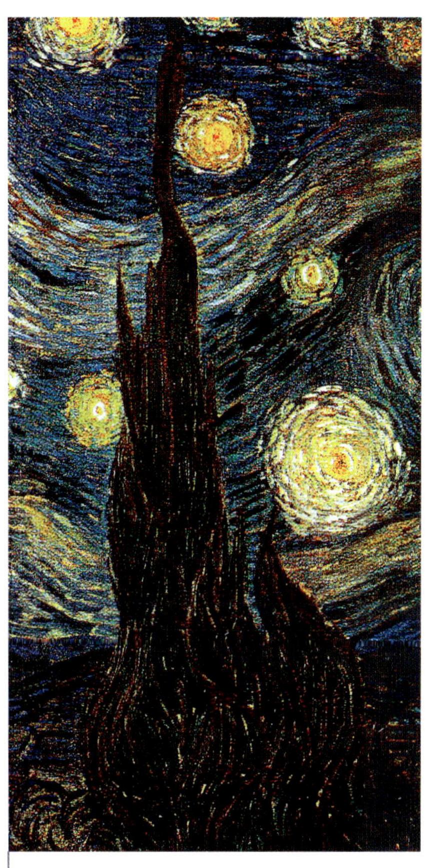

Detail of STARRY NIGHT. *Reproduction from the painting by Vincent Van Gogh, 1889*

Since the Church has served in past centuries as one of the major promoters of mosaic art, it seems fitting that it would also assume a role of responsibility for the survival of this artform in this critical time. Indeed, an initial step in this direction was taken on the occasion of the Jubilee Year 2000 when the Holy See, and precisely the Pontifical Commission for the Cultural Heritage of the Church under the leadership of His Eminence, Cardinal Francesco Marchisano, promoted a workshop entirely dedicated to mosaic craftsmanship in Venice.[2] With the support of the Council of Europe, where I was serving as Holy See delegate, this meeting gathered scholars in art history, archaeology, conservation artists and mosaic craftsmen, from ten different nations and representing the major monotheistic religions in Europe, in order to evaluate the tremendous contribution of this artform for the development of the cultural heritage of mankind, the conditions and needs faced today, in order to assure its development in the future. It became an occasion when a dramatic appeal emerged, especially on the part of the craftsmen themselves, revealing its present-day problematic situation. Our promise then to continue a serious commitment towards an increased enhancement of this tradition finds an additional launching pad in this important exhibition here in New Orleans which has also been conceived to offer a special opportunity in the area of training, particularly aimed at young generations, as an integral part of the event. We hope that it will inspire the spread of initiatives and a deeper consciousness in this country so that it may continue to build upon its outstanding patronage tradition as a fundamental contribution assuring this craftsmanship's actual survival.

The second challenge that we hope will be met by this exhibition concerns our general perception of what the potential of art can be in today's world. In this respect, we can say that there is perhaps a need to reflect upon and even recover those issues proposed precisely by those whom we consider to be the fathers of abstract and contemporary art. Back in 1910 Kandinsky challenged the art world by saying, "Spiritual life of which art is a fundamental component is an ascending and progressive movement... it is a movement of knowledge" [3]. Referring to a well known Ravenna mosaic panel in order to point out the melodic qualities necessary to the making of a compositional entity, he also adds, "Painting is an art and art is not a useless creation of things that vanish in emptiness but it is a force with an aim and it must serve for the development and refinement of the soul..." [4].

There is no doubt that it was the same concern that guided the hands of artistic geniuses and mosaic craftsmen at work inside St. Peter's Basilica 500 years ago. We hope

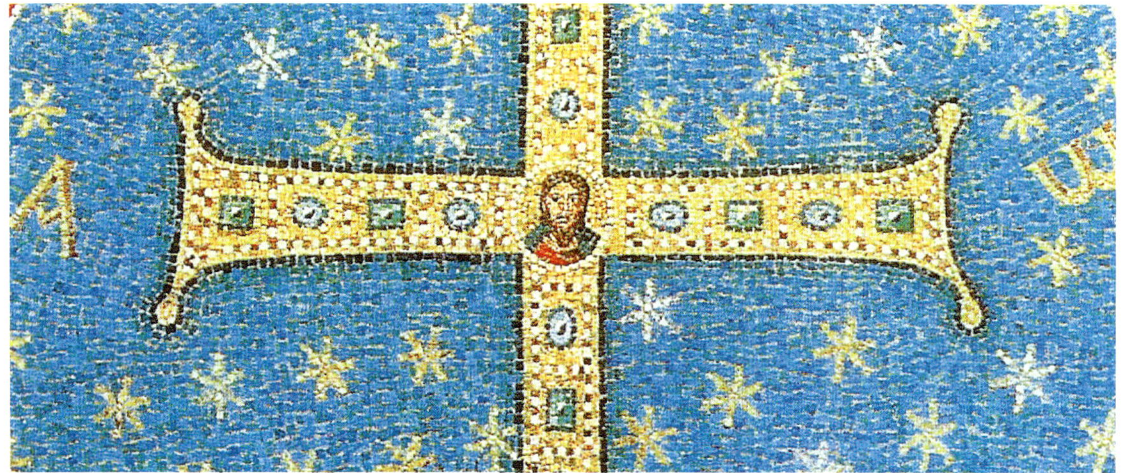

Detail of a Byzantine Cross. Reproduction from apse mosaic, 6th century A.D

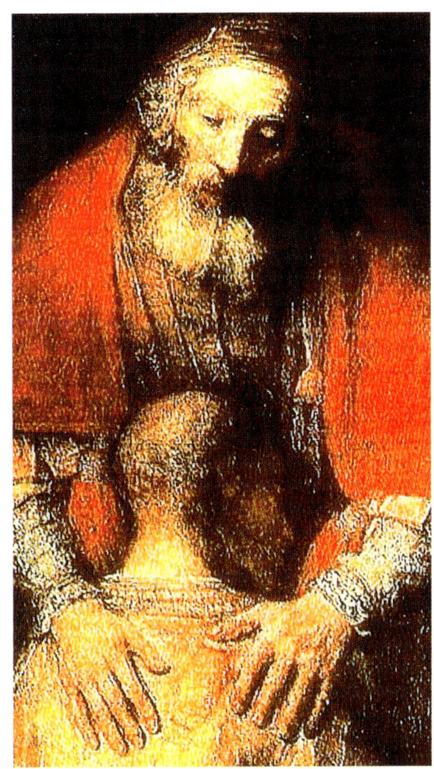

Detail of THE PRODIGAL SON. *Reproduction from detail of the painting by Rembrandt, 1669*

that each visitor of the exhibition may see through the beauty of each individual work on display this precise aim and perceive it, guard it, as a spiritual treasure that can illuminate his/her individual path of life with a deeper appreciation of art as a powerful communication channel of hope, beauty, harmony, leading towards the contemplation of an eternal reality of divine presence.

I would like to take this opportunity to thank all my collaborators at the Fabbrica of St. Peter who have enthusiastically assisted me in the preparation and organization of this exhibition, especially all the mosaic artists of the Vatican Studio, our photographer Mr. Marco Andreozzi, my colleague archaeologist Mr. Pietro Zander; and most of all our superiors, His Eminence Cardinal Francesco Marchisano, Archpriest of St. Peter's Basilica, and His Excellency Archbishop Angelo Comastri, President of the Fabbrica of St. Peter's, for their continued support. Finally a very special thanks to the Archdiocesan community of New Orleans, especially Archbishop Alfred C. Hughes for his trust; Father Gerald L. Seiler, Msgr. Crosby W. Kern and the entire staff at St. Louis Cathedral, Dr. Charles Nolan and the staff at the Catholic Cultural Heritage Center, for their gracious hospitality and assistance, and to everyone who has contributed their efforts to sponsor and assure the success of this unique event.

NOTES:

1. Foundation stones laid on April 18, 1506.
2. Cathedral Workshops on Religious Arts and Crafts - Proceedings. Edindustria: 2003, pp. 29-113.
3. Trans. from Wassily Kandinsky *Lo Spirituale nell'Arte*. Milano: 1989, pp. 20-21.
4. Trans. from Ibid, p. 88.

St. Louis Cathedral/The Old Ursuline Convent A Catholic Cultural Heritage Center

By Dr. Charles Nolan, Archivist and Director of the Office of Cultural Heritage, Archdiocese of New Orleans

The Vatican Mosaic Studio exhibition is hosted by the Catholic Cultural Heritage Center of the Archdiocese of New Orleans. The Center includes two of the city's most historic structures: St. Louis Cathedral and the Old Ursuline Convent, the oldest building in the Mississippi Valley. The exhibition is housed on the first floor of the convent.

In February 2004, Msgr. Crosby W. Kern, the 43rd pastor/rector of St. Louis Cathedral in New Orleans, announced the establishment of St. Louis Cathedral/Old Ursuline Convent: A Catholic Cultural Heritage Center. The Center is administered by Msgr. Kern, assisted by Dr. Charles E. Nolan, archdiocesan archivist and director of the newly-established Archdiocesan Office of Cultural Heritage.

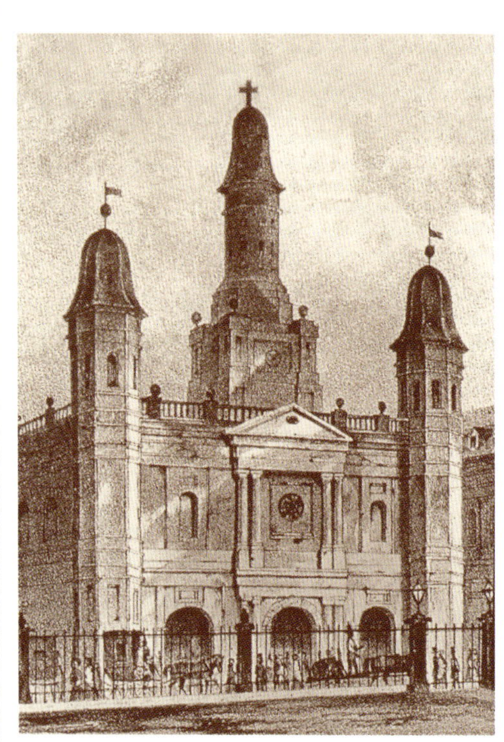

St. Louis Cathedral as rebuilt in 1794

St. Louis Cathedral is the oldest existing Catholic cathedral in continual use in the United States. The first permanent church on this site was completed in 1723. After the devastating 1788 fire, a new church was erected through the generosity of Don Andres Almonester y Roxas and occupied in 1794.

St. Louis Church became a cathedral in 1793 when the vast Diocese of Louisiana and the Floridas was established with Cuban priest Luis Peñalver y Cárdenas as the new diocese's first bishop. The new diocese stretched from Key West Florida northward to the American colonies, across the Gulf Coast, and west of the Mississippi to Texas and Canada.

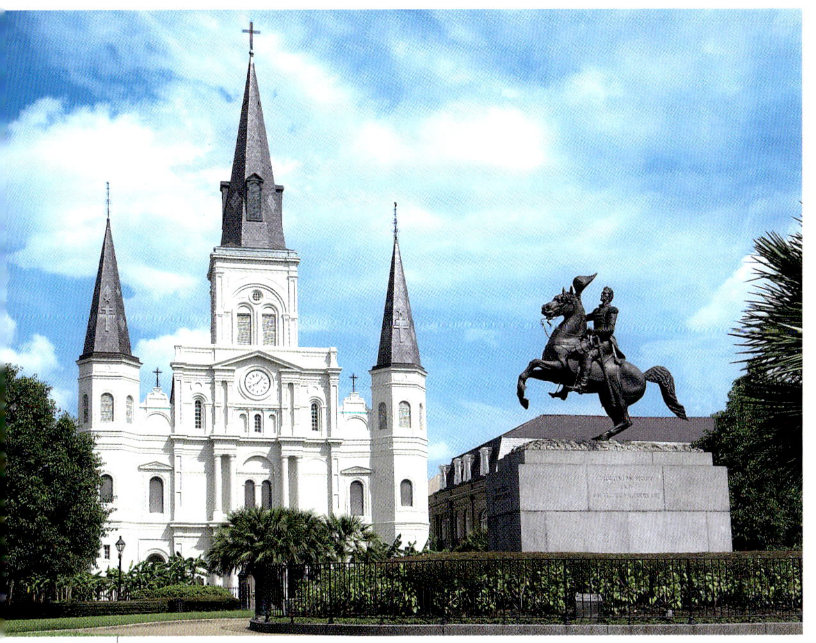

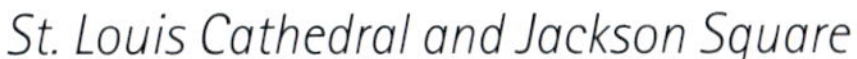

St. Louis Cathedral and Jackson Square

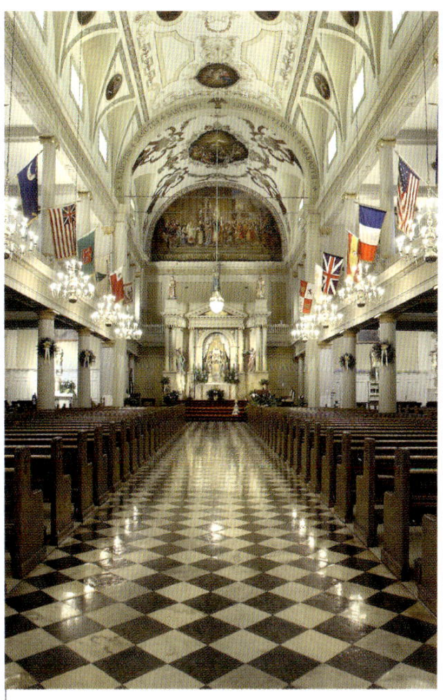

Cathedral center aisle

The present cathedral, almost completely rebuilt and expanded over the 1794 building, was completed in 1851. The cathedral has been the city's center of worship as well as a gathering place for major political, cultural, and social events for more than 280 years.

The first Ursuline nuns, led by Mother Marie St. Augustin Tranchepain from the Rouen convent, arrived in New Orleans in 1727 to take charge of the royal hospital. Since work on their convent had not begun, they first resided at the Kolly House where they immediately opened a day and boarding school. The nuns also began instructing both Native American and African girls and women, laying the foundation for a strong African American presence in the local church.

In 1734, the convent, located on the present grounds but closer to the Mississippi River, was completed. The three story building, built with bricks between timber, soon proved inadequate.

Spanish statue at Ursuline Museum

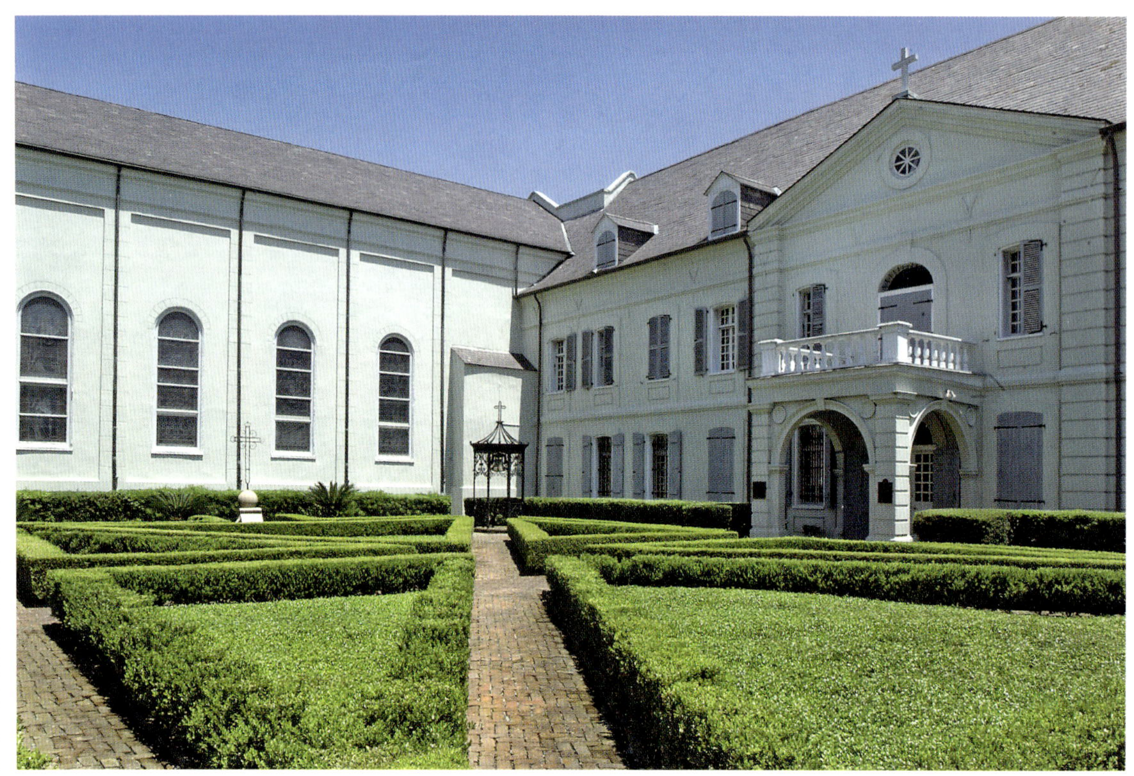

Convent front garden, modeled on early New Orleans garden and designed by Samuel Wilson Jr.

The present convent was authorized by King Louis XV of France in 1745. The nuns moved into the completed convent in 1752 or 1753. This remained their home and the center of their ministry for the next seventy years.

After the Ursulines departed in 1824, the building served as the bishop's and then archbishop's residence (*l'archêveché*), the archdiocesan administration building and chancery, a Catholic boys' school and a public school, the seat of the Louisiana legislature, the residence of the Oblate Fathers serving the Italian community, and the archdiocesan archives. The adjoining St. Mary's Church dates from 1845.

The Archdiocese of New Orleans' Catholic Cultural Heritage Center takes its inspiration and direction from the Pontifical Commission for the Cultural Heritage of the Church. Established in 1988 with Archbishop (now Cardinal) Francesco Marchisano as its first president, the commission directed all Catholic dioceses throughout the world to look upon their archives, libraries, architecture, painting, sculpture, music, etc., as a single sacred heritage, to take the necessary steps to identify and preserve this heritage, and to place this heritage at the service of the local Church's mission of evangelization, catechesis, and education.

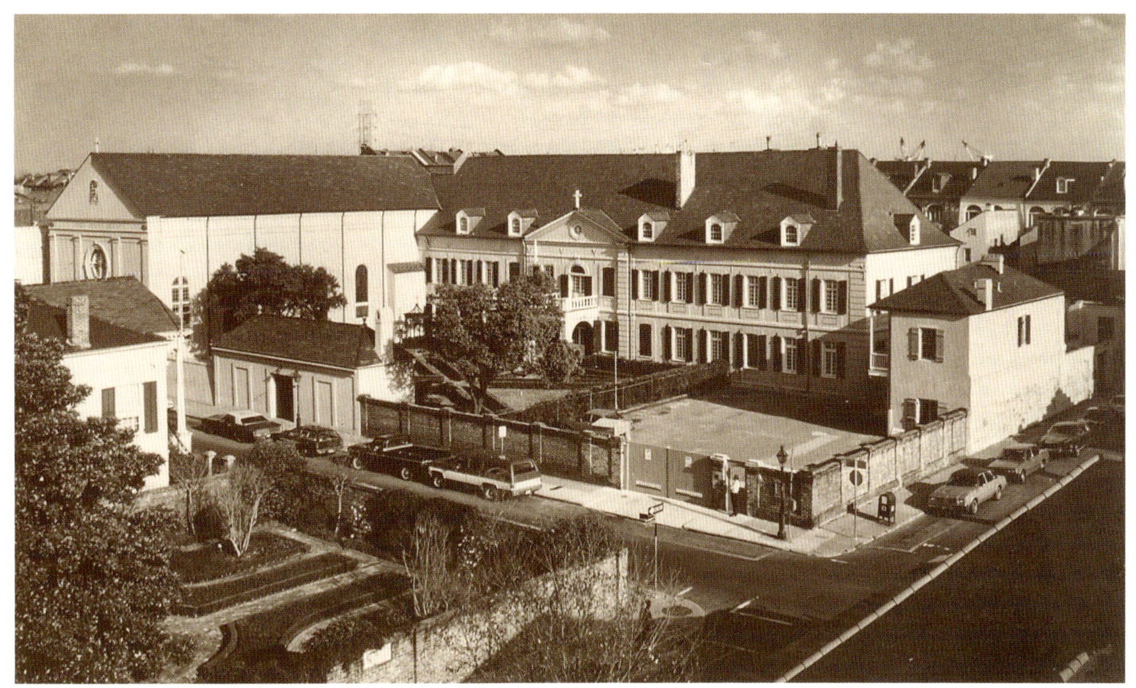

Old Ursuline Convent and St. Mary's after 1970s restoration

The Vatican documents further urge each diocese to establish an appropriate center that would become "an authentic greenhouse, a living center for cultural development" for the entire community. In addition to the cathedral's first St. Joseph Altar on March 17, 2004, in St. Anthony's Garden, the first concerts by some of the world's most renowned organists from France, England, and the United States were inaugurated on the newly-installed Holtkamp organ on April 24, 2005.

On October 1, 2004, Francesco Cardinal Marchisano, the founding president of the Vatican Commission on the Cultural Heritage of the Church and current Archpriest of St. Peter's Basilica in Rome, blessed the newly-opened Catholic Cultural Heritage Center. The first exhibits reflected the city's rich and diverse cultural heritage, not only in the unique architectural beauty of the convent itself, but also in statues, paintings, photographs, sacred vessels, documents, musical instruments, vestments, clocks, maps, school notebooks and science instruments, newspapers, illustrations, letters from Ralph Waldo Emerson and Henry David Thoreau, early Ursuline Academy school books and the ledgers of the St. Louis Church wardens listing the 1755-1756 pew holders. More than 3,500 visitors from all fifty states, the District of Columbia, and forty foreign nations from every section of the globe saw the exhibits during the final three months of 2004.

On August 29, 2005, Hurricane Katrina struck with devastating ferocity at the greater New Orleans area and the Gulf Coast. Both St. Louis Cathedral and the Old Ursuline Convent suffered significant damage. St. Louis Cathedral reopened by candlelight for its first post Katrina Mass on September 19, 2005, although the newly-renovated organ had to be dismantled and sent to the Holkamp studios for major repairs. The Old Ursuline Convent remained closed for seventeen months. The opening day of the Vatican Mosaic Studio exhibition also marks the solemn reopening of the convent.

The Vatican Mosaic Studio exhibition and workshops provide a unique opportunity for the Archdiocesan Catholic Cultural Heritage Center to serve the wider community as an authentic "greenhouse", a living center for cultural development that can spread and strengthen awareness for the conservation and enhancement of the cultural heritage of the Church.

According to common thinking, the word museum recalls to mind a place separated from present day life; an unchanged, static, cold and silent place. The ecclesiastical museum instead should qualify itself as an authentic 'greenhouse', a living center for cultural development that can spread and strengthen awareness for the conservation and enhancement of the cultural heritage of the Church.

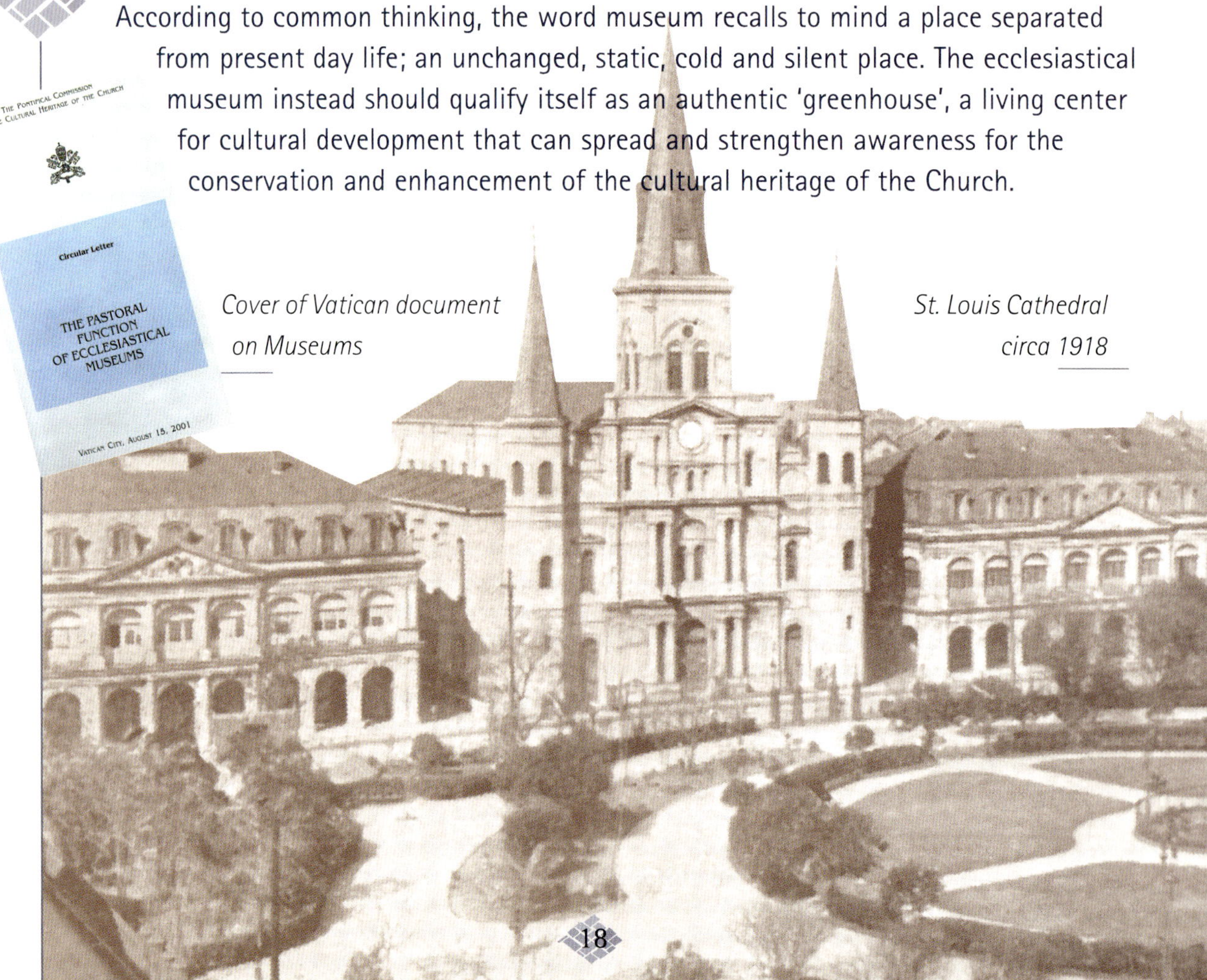

Cover of Vatican document on Museums

St. Louis Cathedral circa 1918

“Mosaics at St. Peter’s Basilica:

An Eloquent Vehicle to Express the Continuity of Sacredness,”

By Dr. Cristina Carlo-Stella

The New Orleans exhibition of mosaic masterpieces produced by the Vatican Mosaic Studio offers an interesting opportunity to evaluate the extraordinary value of the mosaic craftsmanship tradition in connection to the development of the sacred building, the Basilica of Saint Peter, that has launched in regards to it what we may perhaps call a revival period of innovative function and technique. Almost exactly twenty years have passed since the noteworthy publication by Zander which presents a general overview of ancient mosaics inside the Basilica and addresses the delicate issue of attribution of some of these works to the various stages of its construction[1]. However fundamental that study certainly proves to be in order to trace an overall evaluation of the material that has survived to the present day, it does not take into consideration the development of this tradition in relation to the extant traces of this craftsmanship that lie below the foundations of the Basilica and emerge from its equally precious archeological environment underneath. This study wants to honor that earlier publication, with the aim of developing further Zander's analysis by focusing more precisely on this artform's continuity which in fact characterizes the history of this holy site. We hope that our perspective may represent an additional useful contribution towards a truly comprehensive study of all the splendid surfaces that in this technique have served to make the Basilica a unique and precious part of the heritage of mankind.

The over 20,000 visitors who cross the solemn threshold of the magnificent Basilica of Saint Peter each day, as they gaze in awe at the breath-taking huge dimensions of the interior space encapsulated by Michelangelo's magnificent dome, are usually fooled easily by what seems to be painted surfaces decorating the more than 25 altars and chapels, which cover a total area of about 10,000 square meters. The illusionistic potential of artistic creation is eloquently perceived here by human consciousness through one of its most successful and perhaps earliest decorative expressions: mosaic technique. While it was precisely this aspect of the artistic process that was openly criticized by Platonic thought, it is interesting to note that mosaic craftsmanship flourishes in the West at a time, c. mid 4th century B.C., when the study of natural phenomena, conducted by the Aristotelian tradition of empirical analysis, brings about a realistic depiction of the human form that takes into consideration its various temporal stages of existence and spiritual condition[2].

This "*tromp-l'œil*" decorative program devised for the Basilica's interior space was launched in the early 17th century and precisely in 1627 when the altarpiece designed by Cavalier d'Arpino for the chapel of Saint Michael the Archangel was translated in mosaic technique. The project coincided with a time when an increasing fascination for optical phenomenon, resulting also from sophisticated scientific experimentation conducted by artists and architects during this period, would soon transform architectural design into an almost pliable sculptural reality; and sculptural works, through the exquisite refinement of surface textures, into living creatures who long for a state of being that transcends the sensual world. Just a few years before the chapel of Saint Michael was completed, Bernini had begun to propose the challenges of this new approach through masterpieces like the David, Apollo and Daphne[3]. The so called Baroque experience, as we encounter it in Rome and through Bernini's works, makes us conscious of a curious paradox: the mastering of technical virtuosity in the treatment of material surfaces becomes an instrument to induce a sensual transcendency that brings about a comprehension of the world beyond the senses[4]. Just about contemporary to the mosaic decoration being applied to embellish St. Michael's chapel, a visionary universe had begun to snatch the gaze of the faithful in other places of worship, as Lanfranco's spinning vision of the Assumption of the Virgin in Sant'Andrea della Valle. Just a year later painters like Poussin, who cleverly exploited the idealized formal canon accompanying mythological vocabulary, and Rembrandt, re-proposed to the faithful and mankind an introspective attitude towards the human condition in relation to the rest of creation and as a way to achieve that interior harmony essential for spiritual meditation and the perception of the transcendental. Clearly the objectives of the Counter-Reformation as well as the development of an elaborate allegorical vocabulary translated through natural elements encountered in one's personal, daily, and domestic environment, had prepared the terrain for an understanding of mystical experience, which implied refining a perception that overcomes the limits of a purely rational understanding of human existence[5].

The mosaic decorative program designed and applied between 1578[6] and throughout the 1600's (when the central dome, vaults, chapels, the first altars were decorated) - up until 1799, makes the new structure of Saint Peter's Basilica, founded on April 18, 1506, truly unique not only in terms of recuperating the tradition of mosaic craftsmanship associated to Christian sacred places of worship, but also for

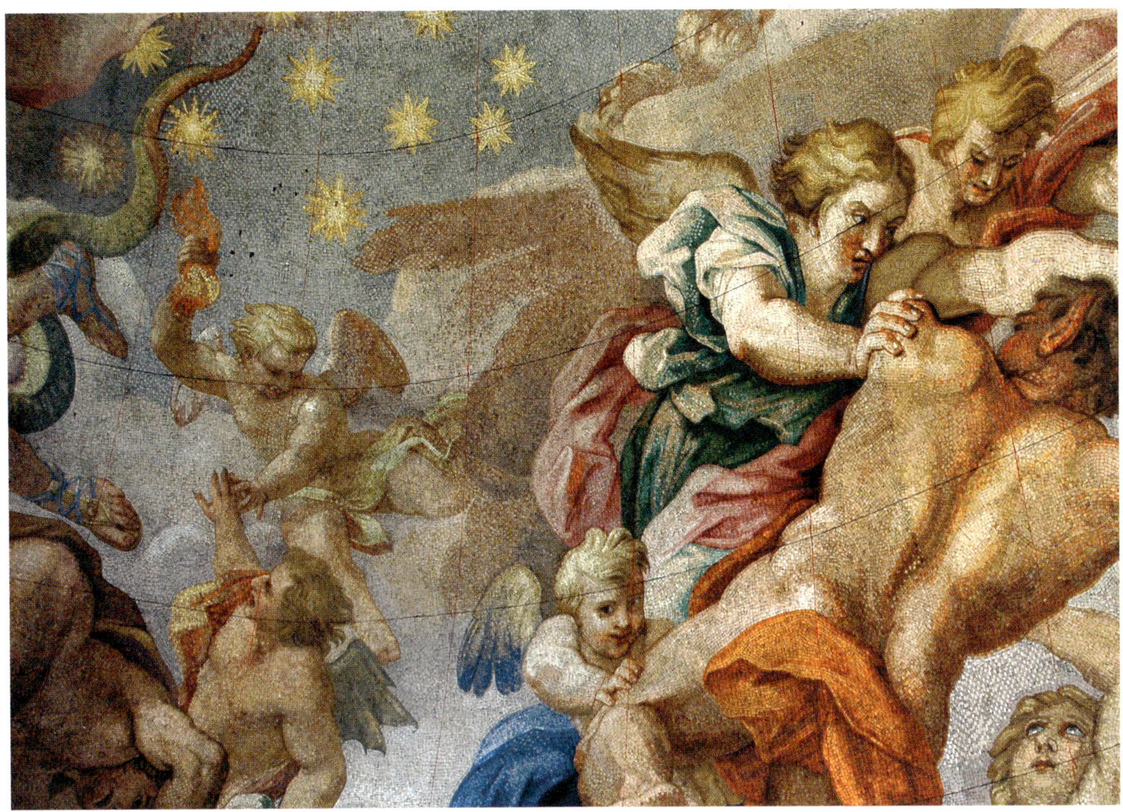

enhancing mosaic decoration precisely for its extraordinary illusionistic potential which also implied innovative techniques of production.

Few of those 20,000 visitors who flow daily through the Basilica's interior space and slowly reach the most sacred area of St. Peter's burial - the so-called confessio - actually realize that the translucent mosaic surfaces forming the ethereal vision depicted in the dome above, in fact represent the epitome of a tradition that has its deeper roots precisely below near St. Peter's burial ground. Indeed mosaic craftsmanship represents for this outstanding sacred site and center of Christian worship, one of the privileged vehicles expressing its unique uninterrupted continuity of veneration, sacredness and faith.

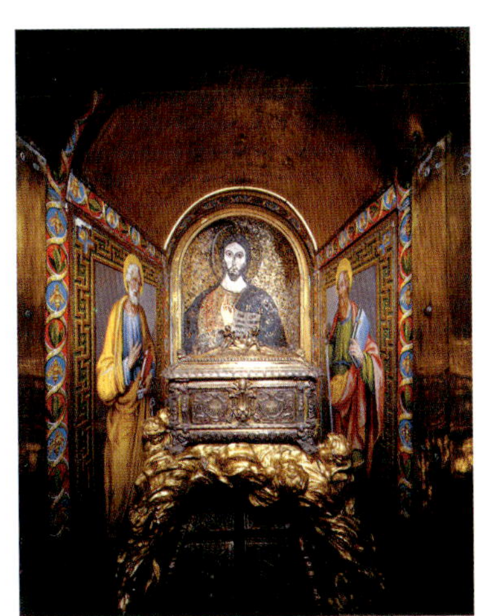

The splendid mosaic panel directly below Bernini's Baldacchino depicting Christ Pantocrator emerges as a visual reference of this extraordinary tradition that has accompanied the history of construction and renovation of this sacred place.

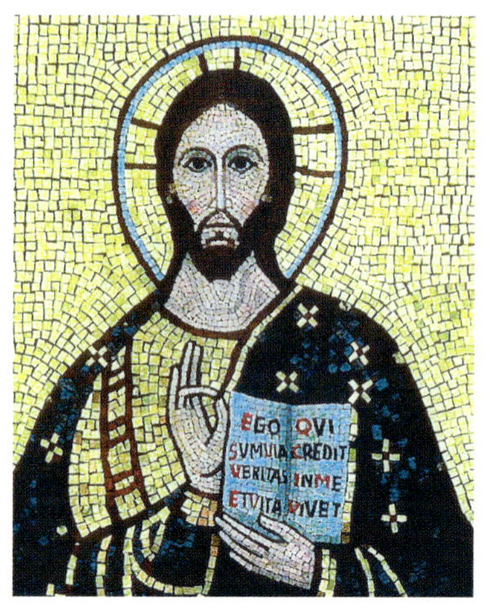

The figure, commissioned by Pope Leo III in the 9th century[7] to mark the burial area where Saint Peter lay, is flanked by the apostles Peter and Paul, following the original design of the composition[8]. While the latter figures were entirely re-designed in the 16th century and fully restored in the following century, the frontal image of Christ is the least restored and thus the most true to the 9th century panel. Its exquisite simplicity of linear facial features and color scheme renders it particularly powerful as the concise message inscribed in the open Book of Revelation He holds which reads "ego sum veritas et vita: qui credit in me vivet". It is an image intended to communicate a powerful message not only to the faithful but to every human being who searches for an understanding of, an assurance in, a life beyond. Clearly the image was especially conceived for this particular area where early Christian martyrs, including the apostle Peter, had shed their blood, trustworthy and perhaps murmuring on their lips this exact promise of salvation.

The so-called "Pallio Niche" housing the Christ Pantocreator image as well as the precious reliquary marking the discovery of the Apostle's mortal remains, emerges as a conjunction point with a lower level below the floor surface. This area underneath, located between the level of the Constantinian basilica and the floor of the present day Basilica, encompassing an ambulatory around the "confessio" proper, forms the Vatican Grottoes[9]. Its adjacent location to the sacred burial ground of the Prince of the Apostles, as well as the major renovation project begun under Pope Clement VIII at the end of the 16th century[10], turned this space into a sacred devotional area suited for liturgical celebrations and personal meditation. At first it was primarily Church leaders and clergy who were allowed to accede, but increasing demands from pilgrims soon led its opening to the general public already by the beginning of the 17th century, on condition of precise strict rules[11]. It is here that one is reminded still today of the original main function of the older Constantinian structure as primarily a sacred funerary environment. The renovation project that transformed these so-called "Grottoes", turned them into a deposit area for the many burials unearthed under the floor of the first Basilica. The meticulous descriptions made by Grimaldi and Torrigio in the 16th – 17th centuries of the original layout of the oratories and chapels together with their decorative features which were unbashfully removed or even demolished for renovation purposes, and gathered here, include touching excerpts concerning the intense devotional piety that permeated this space. Around 1623, Torrigio writes: "many people from across the mountain go there with incredible piety; the Cardinals and Prelates with even more wonderful pleasure, and upon seeing the sacred ancient monuments are filled with celestial consolation; there is no corner they do not want to see, not a single epitaph they do not want to read, no inscription they do not wish to ponder, no sacred image, figure or stone they do not honor by a kiss of devotion, as they are inspired by the sanctity of the venerated Grottoes...."[12]

Numerous fragments of mosaic panels once decorating the oratories, the facades and other interior areas of the Constantinian Basilica found a dignified temporary or permanent abode in the Grottoes. Among these are fragments recorded by Grimaldi in 1606 as belonging to the mosaic cycle decorating the impressive Oratory commissioned by Pope John VII, which were described as "pulcherrime"[13]. From these records one can assume that this cycle presented a rather articulated iconographic program. It included New Testament scenes, scenes from the lives of the Apostles Peter and Paul and two large representations of the Virgin to whom the Oratory was dedicated[14]. Stylistically speaking, the decoration appears to have been particularly elaborate as the mosaic panels were framed by stucco reliefs studded with pagan mythological and allegorical imagery. The juxtaposition of pagan and Christian scenes, as well as the inclusion of an image of the Virgin depicted as imperial queen dressed in plush regal high Byzantine garb, would presumably reveal the direct contribution of Greek mosaic craftsmen. This hypothesis would seem quite plausible in fact considering Pope John's personal upbringing and background. Son of a Byzantine official who was the curator of the imperial palace on the Palatine hill, and educated in Constantinople, this Pontiff soon became known for his virtuous discreetness[15].

We are fortunate that his image has survived in a fragment that once belonged to the mosaic panel above the Oratory's altar. He is depicted donating a model of the Oratory to the Virgin Imperial Queen who would have been represented in prayerful pose. Pope John considered himself a simple "*servus sanctae Mariae*". As an expression of his deep devotion to the Mother of God, he commissioned major decorative programs and sacred images in her honor in two other major churches in Rome, Santa Maria Antiqua and Santa Maria in Trastevere. In the former case, he employed skilled Greek artists who endowed their figures with an exquisite subtle modelling recalling Hellenistic impressionist techniques associated to the Justinianic figure canon[16]. If in fact the beginning of the 8th century seems on one hand to constitute, also for this reason, a distinct phase of its own[17] which sought to synthesize the experience of the earlier Byzantine tradition in the West, one can detect in the Pope's image perhaps a slightly different approach[18]. The mosaic artist seems to focus on a portrait revealing his unique meek and sensitive personality, while formal considerations seem to be only a secondary concern. Even the peculiar iconographic traits associated to the image, like the square nimbus which can be traced directly to that Greek tradition of religious imagery associated to episcopal figures, as shown in at least a couple of examples in Paris and Salonika - precious models like the Coptic painting at the Bibliotheque Nationale in Paris[19] or the mosaic panel depicting two male donors from the church of Hagios Demetrios in Salonika and dating to the second half of the 7th century[20] - here can be interpreted as features further emphasizing his humble character (personality).

The other fragments that have been associated with the mosaic program in the Oratory[21] reveal different hands at work and qualitative standards: from the most schematic renderings in the fragments depicting presumably Saint Peter preaching, and the scene of the child Jesus bathing now located in the gallery of Clement VIII to a more sophisticated and painterly rendition in the fragment presumably depicting Christ entering Jerusalem.

Indeed, the faithful approaching the interior of the original Basilica built by Emperor Constantine around 320 A.D. must have had the impression of entering a close replica of the heavenly Jerusalem. According to the Liber Pontificalis, the interior appeared spectacularly brilliant. In addition to the natural lighting provided by the clerestory windows that studded the 90 meters long central nave, 32 silver candelabras shed a more diffused light which became further potentialized by the 50 candelabras in the side aisles. The huge apse facing westward was covered with gold mosaics with a solid gold cross placed at the center above a silver gilt altar studded with four hundred precious stones[22]. One can just intuitively imagine the effects of the flickering light rays bouncing off the ceiling's gold tesserae and blending with the silver tinted flashes of light radiating from the altar's surface together with the rainbow colored lights refracted from its precious inlays. While this area represented the epitome of this pseudo-paradisiac vision, the interior space leading to this magnificent climax revealed other innovative features.

As we know, the Constantinian Basilica, designed to encompass the venerated sacred area where the Apostle Peter was believed to be buried, proposed the first example of a basilican planned martyrium shrine[23]. For this purpose the standard utilitarian and polyvalent basilican architectural model becomes more elaborate in design by an additional horizontal area, or transept, delineating the liturgical area proper, initially reserved for the clergy and those faithful who wished to meditate, from the covered graveyard area embraced by the nave space where crowds, including the relatives of the deceased, came to pay homage and conduct the funeral rites by the tomb of their loved ones. The transition between the nave and the transept area was marked by a triumphal arch, which proclaimed symbolically by its form a victory sign of life over death. This programmatic layout of the interior space that foresaw the fusion of funerary and liturgical environments united harmoniously under one architectural form must have been so directly eloquent and incisive to the minds and souls of those gathered. It must have impressed immediately in pilgrims another dogmatic message regarding the essential meaning of the ecclesial community and its function, a community that must believe and bring hope in an eternal life, a community that is collegial and participative in Peter's mission.

Mosaic decoration was not only confined to the far end apse area. The semi-dome was covered by a mosaic cycle that included a long and interesting inscription citing the year 337 as the year of completion[24]. The cycle underwent major restoration during the first half of the 7th century until it was entirely replaced by Pope Innocent III in the 13th century with a composition that seems to have been modelled almost exactly after the original model, if one considers valid comparisons with decorative cycles which appear on other precious extant works like the well-known Pola casket[25]. In 1592, the entire mosaic cycle was demolished by the will of Pope Clement[26]. Approximately a century after the completion of the building, a mosaic program was commissioned by Pope Leo I for the facade. No fragments survive from these cycles, yet a painted reproduction of Pope Innocent's commission is found in the Vatican Grottoes[27]. The iconographic scheme includes a Christ in majesty scene flanked by the two apostles Peter and Paul, and a more elaborate allegorical composition focusing on an Agnus Dei image accompanied by the personification of the Roman Church and the Church of Hebrews.

One other major mosaic cycle needs to be recalled that leads us back to the narthex area, an area that became rather problematic for this extraordinary construction feat that had to consider solutions for the sloping terrain of the Vatican hill. As in the previous cases no major fragment survives from this composition, but again we can deduce its original appearance from a painted replica found on the eastern wall of the Partorienti chapel in the Grottoes[28]. The work, often referred to as the "Navicella mosaic" and presumably executed by the mid 13th century by Giotto himself or his workshop, depicts the Gospel recount of the miracle of Saint Peter walking on water on a windy day during a fishing outing with the other apostles.

It is a scene in which another clear message of hope could have been deduced by the faithful admiring it, the same message that not long ago resounded in the words of Saint Peter's successor, Pope John Paul II: "do not be afraid" which also implies a strenghtening of faith and trust, the assurance of the Saviour's presence even when confronted with stormy waters; and invites to an internal harmony which can perceive and experience the miracle of transcendency which turns the impossible possible.

As we just mentioned, the building project devised for the Constantinian basilica was not an easy feat but certainly required exceptional skill and experience in architectural and engineering fields. Ensuring that a sacred building of this size may set stable foundations on a sloping surface, while respecting the legal provisions for the pre-existing funerary monuments that characterized this suburban area with the intention of incorporating a part of them within the sacred structure, must have seemed impossible conditions indeed for the success of this demanding project. But determination and perhaps even a good amount of courage in taking difficult decisions, led to the levelling off process of the terrain which necessarily implied cutting the roofs of the higher lavish funerary monuments of aristocratic family burials, and planning an impressive landfill of terrain measuring approximately 8 meters deep to cover the gaps created by the sloping outline of the hill site. It meant in the end, burying beneath the ground the pre-existing 22 funerary mausolea found in this construction area, containing an overall total of 1,000 burials, for almost 1,700 years.

The earliest area of the necropolis included buildings which were aligned parallel, covering a surface beneath the Basilica's central nave that extended from the papal altar to the chapels of the Choir and the Holy Sacrament. They delineated an earthen pathway close to Emperor Nero's circus – the site of martyrdom for numerous Christians including Saint Peter. Around the second half of the 2nd century A.D. the circus fell into disuse. Its abandonment allowed the construction of a second row of funerary buildings in front of the oldest sepulchres. A third street ran parallel to the earlier two pathways that climbed the Vatican hill, behind the row of monuments that were arranged along the first path[29].

The mausolea present the typical model of Imperial chamber tombs built by those whom we would consider to be nowadays middle class people, that is, as small houses equipped with doors, doorposts, facade windows, terraces and fences, similar to those found in the famous Isola Sacra graveyard on the outskirts of Rome. The construction material employed for building the tombs was either red brick or yellow brick and the size range varied from small ones that contained one single family burial, to larger ones that were often passed on to other family groups. The latter could contain as many as 170 burials (as in the case of Mausoleum H known as of "the Valerii").

The front door opened inwards giving access to an interior, surmounted usually by a cross vault[30], that contained in most cases both burials by cremation - as indicated by the small circular niches along the walls that served as display cases for the cinerary urns placed there; and burials by inhumation placed within larger wall openings in a lunette design usually along the bottom wall area. Inhumation burials were also placed beneath the floor surface where often holes were interspersed to pour the traditional libations that were part of the funerary rites conducted by the relatives of the deceased.

The size and the type of external and internal decoration of these buildings obviously depended upon the financial resources of the owners. It is perhaps important to keep in mind that the necropolis was an open-air ground originally and not an underground area as it became after its burial under the land fill needed for the construction of the Constantinian basilica. This meant that the buildings were caressed by natural daylight that also infiltrated through the windows often inserted into the facade above the doorways.

Some of the mausolea were accidentally broken into as the Constantinian basilica's floor surface was dismantled as part of the renovation project that led to the building of the new Basilica in the 16th century. Descriptions recorded in the 1570's give an idea of the excitement and surprise that accompanied these discoveries which must have certainly contributed to enhance the patronage tradition of the antiquarian heritage by the papal court[31].

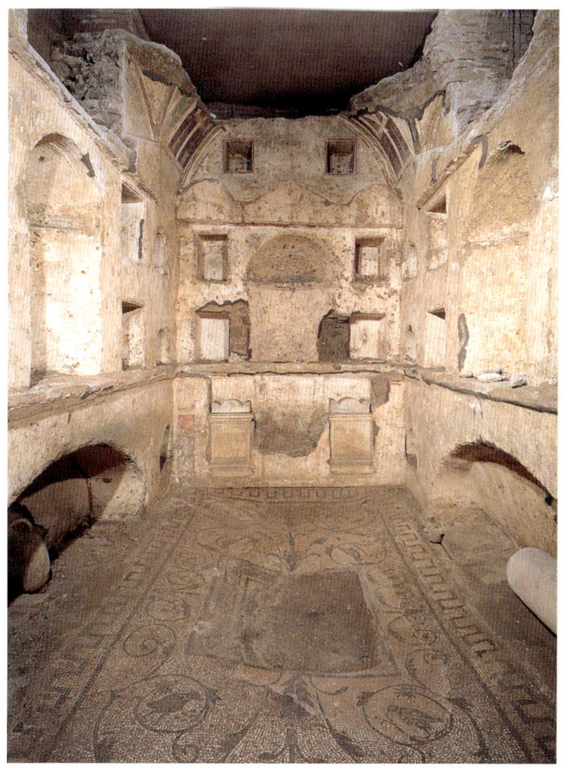

It is at this core level, within the necropolis proper, that we encounter the roots of that mosaic tradition that was to flourish and develop in the following centuries in Christian sacred liturgical and ritual spaces.

Nine mausolea display this artform offering a myriad of different types, techniques, subject matter and meanings. The most impressive mosaic cycles found here cover not only pavement surfaces, but in an exceptional case also facade and vault areas, making these truly precious examples in the history of funerary art both for their stylistic as

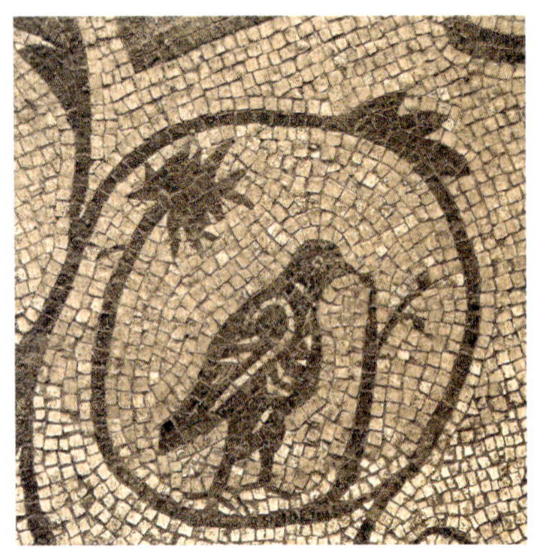

well as iconographic value.

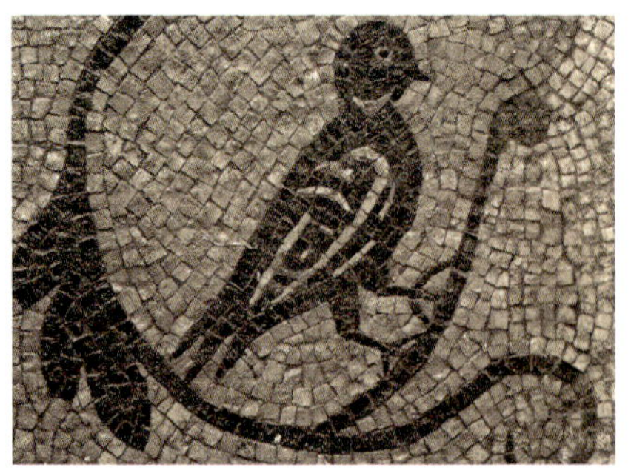

Pavement mosaic surfaces, or traces of them, have been found in eight mausolea dating from the late first half to mid 2nd century. The decoration is laid in tesserae of various sizes depending on the pattern or composition depicted, and usually maintaining a chromatic preference for black and white patterns. Only in one case can we definitely detect the insertion of one or two polychrome areas within the black and white composition. These pavement examples stretch to cover the entire floor surface and include in some cases the emblematic tradition in the center of the composition. The majority of the examples found present a rather traditional juxtaposition of registers

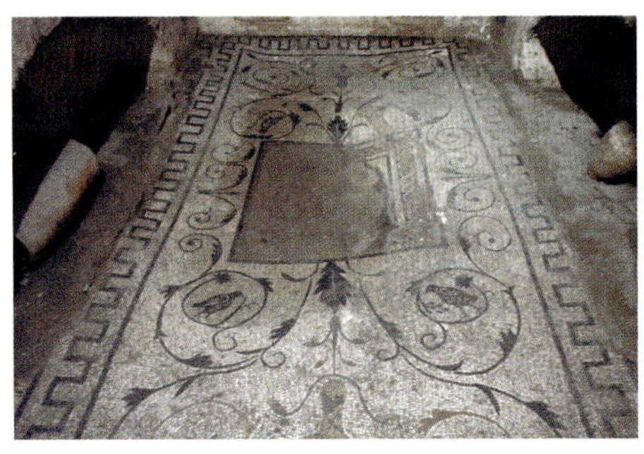

with vegetal motifs alongside others with geometric patterns. There are no examples of floor surfaces entirely decorated with one principle illusionistic geometric tapestry scheme. One of the recurrent vegetal motifs is the "vine and foliate" pattern whereby the surface is covered with stems intertwining or flanking the representations of funeral vessels used for libations. The compositions follow a specific orientation and can include motifs that are arranged in opposite reflection to accommodate also a view from the back wall. Stylized depictions of different bird species may be embraced by these elegant vegetal spirals which if analyzed closely reveal at times some naturalistic features.

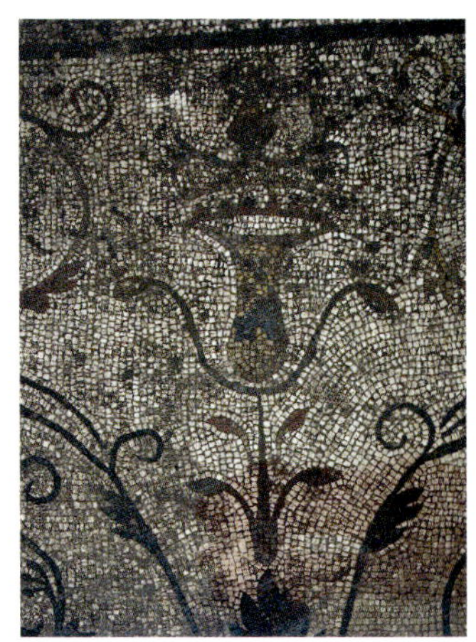

Mausoleum I

The most elaborate black and white pavement composition is found in Mausoleum I, the tomb that was last to be discovered in 1946[32]. The tomb presents an elaborate program of wall paintings characterized by elegant and delicate linear depictions of naturalistic motifs:

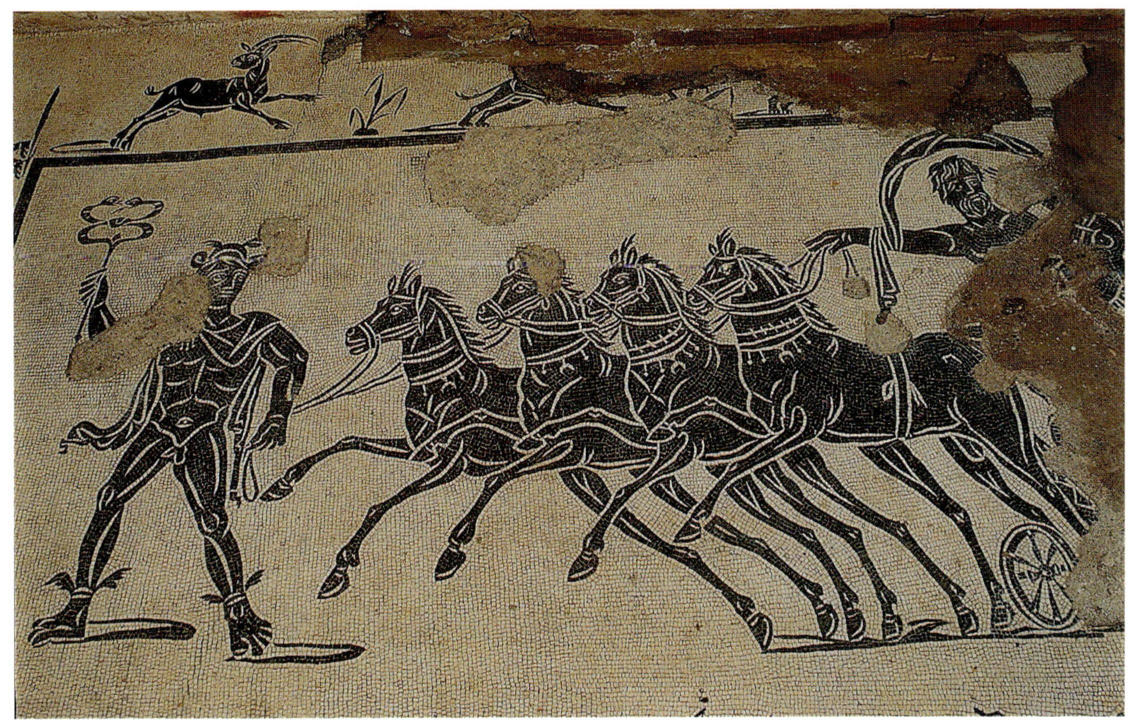

flowers, birds, vases filled with fruit or flowers; that in a dim-lighted interior must have seemed almost ethereal as they emerge against a predominant white background surface. A variety of animal species are represented here with extraordinary realism, as for example the parrot, the duck, a ferocious tiger, or the magnificent large peacocks whose fluffy and colourful feathers are skillfully outlined with extraordinary detail. These motifs, as well as the human figures represented which reveal through the careful rendering of their anatomical proportions and stance late classical models, seem to point to the work of a highly skilled painter or team of painters.

To accompany this almost paradisiac naturalistic environment, the floor mosaic composition depicts a well known mythological scene, the Abduction of Persephone into the Underworld. The subject fits well in a funerary context since it can be interpreted on an allegorical level to symbolize the physical abduction of a soul into the afterworld[33]. Two figures can be easily identified: Pluto depicted as the horrifying charioteer of an energetic quadriga; and, on his right, the standing figure of Mercury holding delicately the caduceus with his right hand. They are made out in black tesserae with highlights in white and silhouetted against an illusionistic field of a white tesserated background, recalling the mosaic pavement tradition in Rome at the beginning of the third century[34] (Roger Ling, *Ancient Mosaics*, British Museum Press, 1998). Below and surrounding them in this central panel, flowers are depicted in black tesserae, sporadically dispersed on the ground. This same floral motif is reechoed

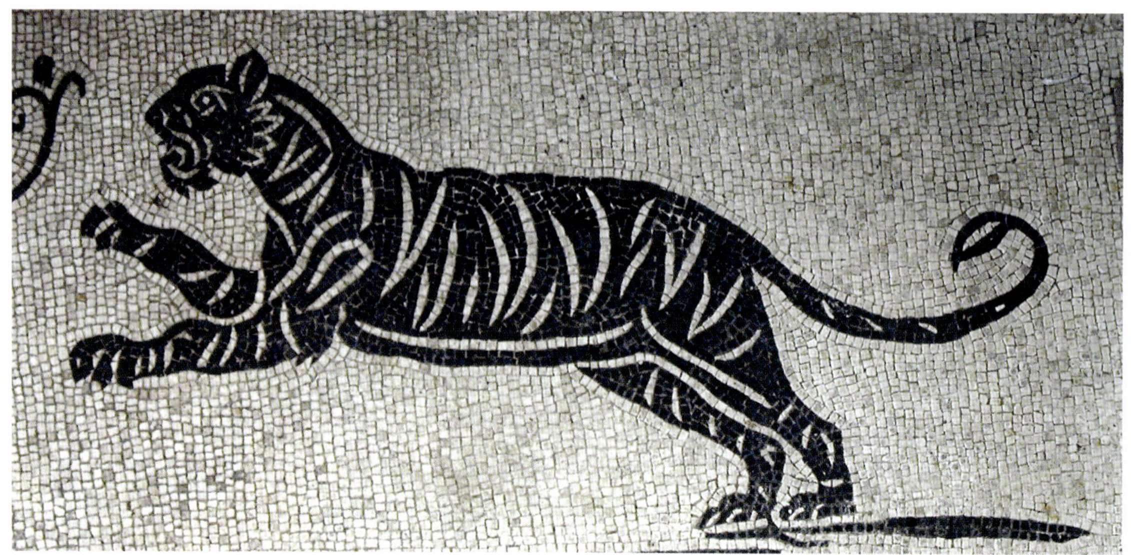

pictorially on the walls' bottom register, thus creating a visual harmony of spatial unity between the pavement and wall surfaces.

The central panel is framed by a border decorated with animal motifs alluding to a hunting scene. The rather massive tigers and slender deer are portrayed standing on their own short ground line from where they either jump in sudden attack of their prey or launch themselves fleeing swiftly from their savage attackers. Their vivacious and energetic character is expressed through a rather naturalistic rendering of their body profiles where stylized striations of highlights made out in white tesserae, marking either the muscle structure or the natural decoration along their bodies also blend to form attractive abstract patterns.

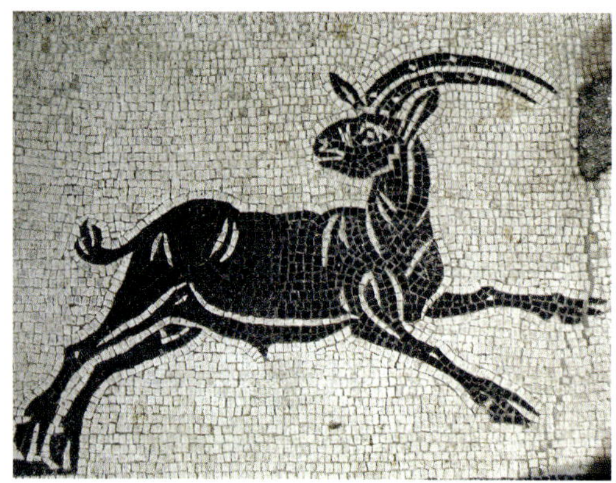

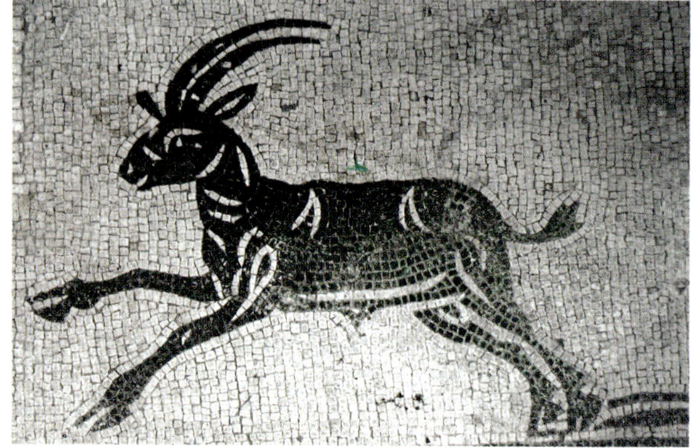

The Mercury figure on the left is portrayed in frontal pose, characterized by a rather heavy and stubby profile in which proportions seems to have been understood in a rather clumsy manner. What emerges here is perhaps more a concern to portray the overall forceful strength of the abduction act through the rather heavy and massive

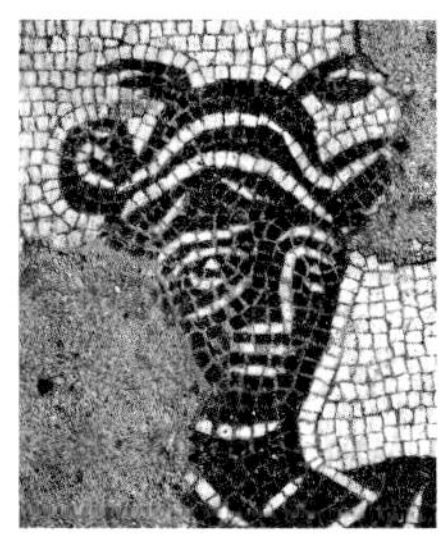

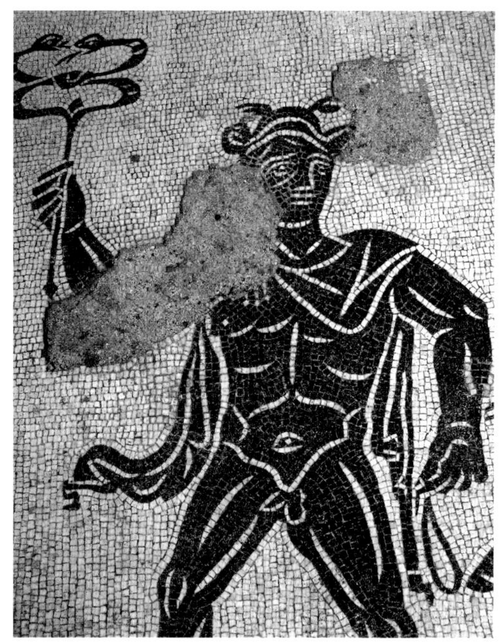

bodies of its protagonists where anatomical detail is just schematically indicated. Even the facial features of both figures are rather crudely delineated revealing a rather impressionist interpretation of their portraits, if compared with the more naturalistic curvilinear lines used to characterize the glance of the deer in the hunting frieze. Nevertheless, the ability of the mosaic artist or artists to deal with delicate design is perhaps best exemplified by the slender profile of the kantharos vase placed between the confronted tigers.

Again we can detect clearly that a strong contrast was intended to be portrayed here between the ferocious strength of the animals, or of nature, and the graciousness of a container whose function in libation ceremonies could have assigned to the object a symbolic meaning as a bearer of nourishment or fertility to the life beyond. One is reminded of the transcription of this iconographic motif in Byzantine mosaic programs decorating ecclesial apsidal spaces as for example in the Church of San Vitale in Ravenna, or in St. Apollinare in Classe[35]. The same holds true for the hunting scene motif that finds a certain popularity from Early Christian times and well into the Byzantine periods, as recalled in a pavement mosaic from the Church at Kabr-Hiram in Lebanon[36]. But one should also recall the popularity of both motifs in funerary art belonging to the classical and Italic/Etruscan traditions. While the latter should in fact be considered more often as a stylistic undercurrent throughout the Roman artistic consciousness, this phenomenon involving the persistent return of specific motifs may be read here as an indication of that modular approach which by the late 2nd century signalled the disintegration of the classical canon and introduced the development of that late antique consciousness which easily penetrated into the Christian artistic syntax[37].

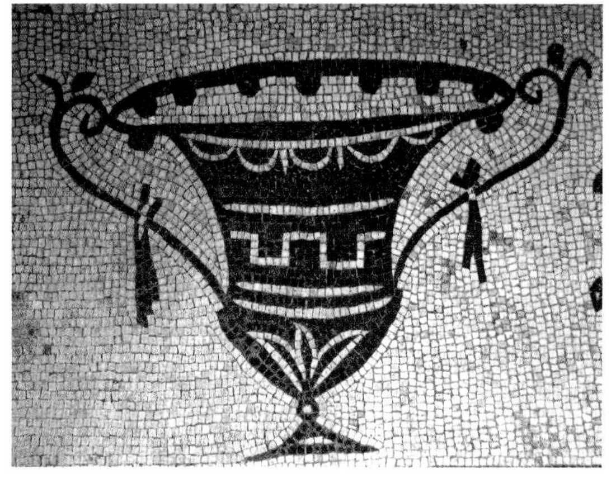

A mythological subject matter can also be detected in a mosaic panel located on the facade of Mausoleum Phi, so-called of the Marci family since it was commissioned, according to the extant inscription, by a certain Quintus Marcius Hermes and his wife Marcia Thraso[38]. Both their portraits have been recorded for posterity in the splendid frieze decoration of the magnificent sarcophagus found in the middle of this chamber tomb. The mythological scene is located under the large facade window and above the doorpost. Executed around the beginning or mid 3rd century, thus not much later than the Persephone pavement composition in Mausoleum I, this splendid panel calls to mind the stylistic and technical virtuosity that often accompanied the emblemata tradition. In addition, it offers an attractive introductory glimpse of the elegant richness of the decorative program that pervades the wall and pavement surfaces of the cross-vaulted interior of this extraordinary funerary chamber. Indeed, mythological subject matter emerges here as the principal source of inspiration for the cycle of wall paintings that decorate the arcosolia inside, which included scenes and figures that have been identified as the Judgement of Paris, Leda – Venus and the swan, the return of Ariadne to Naxos, Hercules and Alcestis, Vesta, Mars and Rea Silva, Nereids and haloed Silenuses[39]; as well as for the high relief decoration of the sarcophagus recalled above which included Dionysiac scenes[40]. Between these decorated arcosolia are zoomorphic representations – ducks, peacocks, marine monsters - which often peak through the elegant floral motifs that stud the wall surfaces.

Certainly such a rich decorative program would indicate the owners' wealth and the employment of an exceptionally skilled team of artists. The polychromatic mosaic emblemata on the facade gives further evidence of this, considering the high quality of its technical execution and refined choice of subject matter. The scene, executed in relatively small colored tesserae, has been identified as the plot devised by the bacchantes on Mount Cithaeron against the King of Thebes, Pentheus, who opposed the Dionysiac cult[41]. A connection to the Dionysiac relief decorating the sarcophagus found inside would possibly reveal some sort of affiliation of the owner to the Dionysiac rites. Only the left half of the composition survives depicting two bacchantes holding sharp daggers in their right hand in the act of shaking a tree against whose trunk a bulky tiger has launched itself energetically while gazing upward evidently waiting for the fall of the victim presumably hidden in the tree. The figures are characterized by harmonious proportions revealed by a careful rendering of their contraposto pose which ensures momentary balance in the immediacy of an energetic action springing forward from the standing leg.

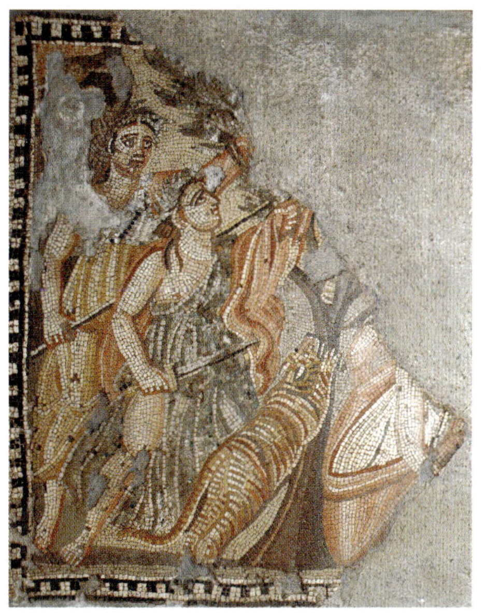

The figures are superbly modelled not only by the drapery here carefully depicted through a cascade of folds outlined by subtle gradations of colored hues (tesserae), but also by this same chiaroscuro effect applied to the facial areas. The same virtuosity, on technical and stylistic levels, can be seen in the depiction of the tiger's dorsal area where the fur skin has become a palette of dozens of different hues, striated to form a kaleidoscopic abstract carpet, that at a distance melts in a rainbow of lights and darks modelling the figure according to a keen naturalistic canon. The tiger is projected against the tree in a clear foreshortening attempt which however seems to have met some difficulties, as the rendition of the head seems too small in comparison to the bulky depiction of the rest of the body. The location of the panel below the window would have permitted a peculiar quality of light on these colored surfaces which would have made them particularly dazzling and bright. Certainly an overall concern for luminosity represented here the major criteria behind the selection of technique and type of mosaic panel for the facade. If one looks closely at the tesserae applied in these polychromatic works, one notices that they were not polished completely smooth to the same surface level in order that their inclinations at different angles would have allowed the refraction of light forming a sparkling effect of colors which no painted surface would have been able to portray.

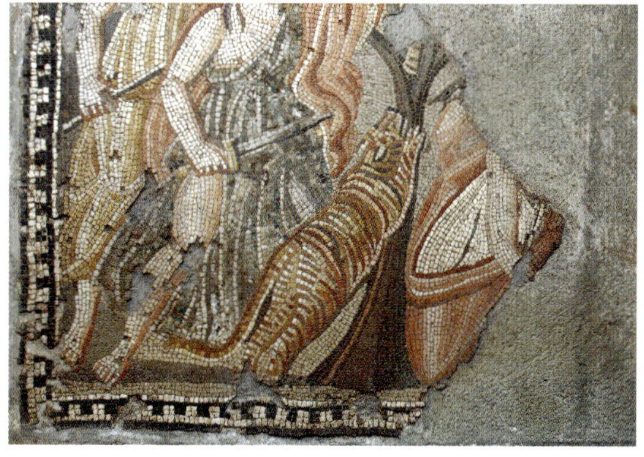

It is quite evident that the mosaic craftsman had a high level of pictorial skill, or perhaps it might have been a painter who translated his talent in mosaic craftsmanship. It is interesting to note that this work, as well as the lushious interior pictorial cycle, was commissioned for a tomb chamber that is located in the area housing also the Mausoleum of the Egyptians. The reference to the Dionysiac cult recorded visually in the Marci Mausoleum is flanked by the former that includes iconographic references to the Isis cult[42]. One can not exclude that the mosaic craftsman and the team of painters employed by Quintius Marcius Hermes came from either the eastern part of the Roman Empire that extended to include Greece, Egypt and Asia Minor. It was in fact at Antioch that the polychrome tradition gained fame for the baroque polychromatic effects of its compositions. This same tradition was also popular in Roman Africa where during approximately this same period a preference seems to have developed for exotic hunt scenes of which examples have also been found in Rome at the Esquiline hill[43].

One other emblemata polychrome panel survives this time inside and on the north wall of Mausoleum Chi. Only a fragment is now extant representing a male figure of uncertain identity[44]. Nevertheless, we encounter here the same type of superb modelling achieved through the chiaroscuro effect produced by the kaleidoscopic range of subtle hues, revealing once again a hand that has mastered almost to perfection the painterly style.

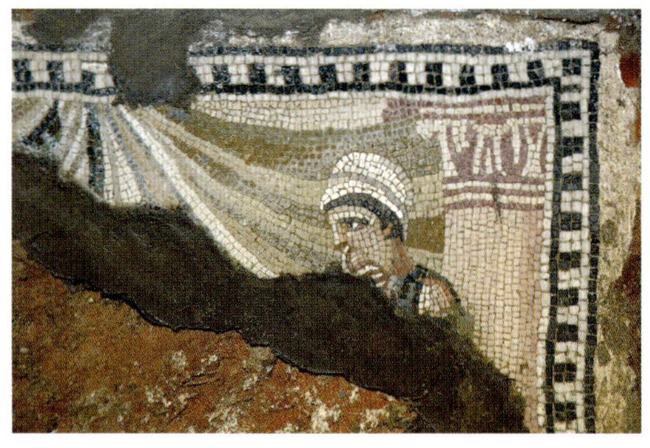

These precious examples discussed so far fit well in that tradition of mosaic wall and ceiling decoration that seems to have been developed exclusively by the Roman artistic consciousness and especially for particular environments that included the flow of water, such as the nymphae, the public termae or private baths[45]. We can deduce therefore that it was indeed the luminous quality of this type of decoration, the play of reflected and refracted lights from the water surfaces, that was considered its particularly attractive feature and which led to its exploitation in order to create extremely lavish and rich interiors as recorded by Seneca. Elaborate examples of wall and vault mosaic surfaces embellished magnificent palatial complexes as Nero's Domus Aurea, Hadrian's villa at Tivoli, or monumental public structures like the Baths of Caracalla, the Baths at Baiae. But we also find application of this technique in domestic interiors at Herculaneum[46], on the Quirinal hill in Rome[47], and finally in funerary environments as in the columbarium of Pomponius Hylas in Rome dating from the 2nd quarter of the 1st century[48]. The Vatican necropolis example from Mausoleum Chi can thus be read as a precious reference demonstrating the continuity of this latter tradition.

If the panel from Mausoleum Chi reminds us of the use of mosaic decoration for interior wall surfaces in funerary environments, the splendid decorative program found inside Mausoleum M represents an exquisite example of this type of mosaic decoration applied to vault areas. This relatively small Mausoleum was previously opened and seen in 1574 during the construction of a small area in front of the high altar of old Saint Peter's Basilica[49]. A rather touching motivation sponsored its construction, as it was built by a mother and father, Julia Palatina and Maximus, for their small boy Julius Tarpeianus who died at an early age of one year, nine months and 27 days[50]. Two burial stages can be recorded in fact inside this chamber tomb: an early cremation tomb that would coincide with the burial of the owners' son, followed by inhumation tombs located under the floor that record the use of this same tomb in the beginning of the 3rd century. Similarly we can distinguish two types of decoration covering its wall surfaces: in the lower register spanning from the floor surface to the inferior half of the wall surface a painted geometric motif, comprised of large diamonds containing a circle and vertical rectangles; and a polychrome mosaic decoration starting from the upper half of the wall surface and comprising the entire vault. The geometric motif on the lower part of the wall would recall the well-known pseudo-marble patterns included in the decorative canon belonging to the wall painting tradition. However, the pattern depicted here stands out for its translation in the classical four color scheme formula (white, yellow, red and black) and for its illusionistic quality conveyed by the superimposition of these geometric forms against a white background.

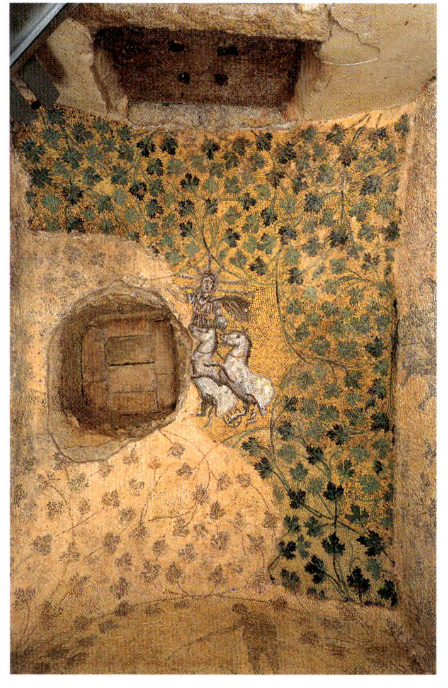

But it is the mosaic decorative cycle stretched out to unite the upper walls and ceiling that further enhances the uniqueness of this extraordinary funerary chamber. The entire iconographic program reveals an exclusive choice of Christian themes[51]: on the west wall a Good Shepherd figure, on the east wall the biblical figure Jonah emerging from the mouth of the whale, on the rear north wall a fisherman; and at the center of the vault a cross-haloed male beardless figure riding a quadriga. The

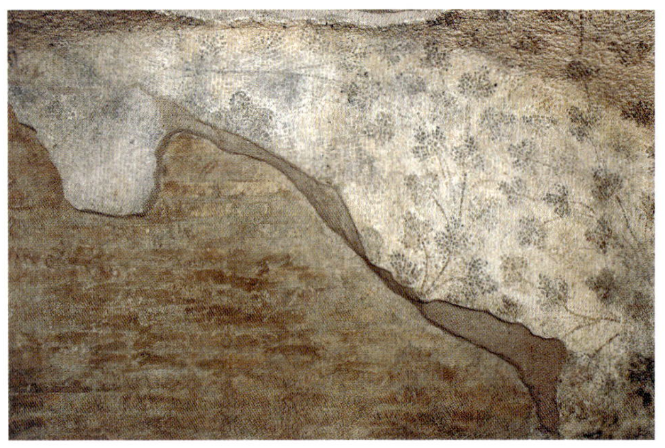

figures are delineated against a golden ochre background which imparts an intense luminosity to the interior and at the same time projects these images in a transcendental atmosphere imbuing them with symbolic meaning. This same atmosphere welcomes a splendid naturalistic rendering of young and vigorous vine scrolls studded by a cascade of fleshy leaves that envelop all the figurative scenes.

Only the bust of the shepherd figure has survived on the west wall – the direction of sunset, but the profile of the lamb placed upon his shoulder is clearly visible. The biblical scene, oriented on the east wall - the direction of sunrise - represents the moment when Jonah has just emerged from the viscous mouth of a large whale, here depicted as a ferocious marine monster with a potent undulating tail, and is being rescued by two fishermen on a boat. On the rear wall the fisherman figure is depicted standing on a small cliff in the act of lifting his fishing rod which has caught one large fish while another flees in the opposite direction. The latter representation has been interpreted in various ways either as a symbolic reference to the rescue of the deceased soul by the Fisherman of Salvation – recalling the writings of Clement of Alexandria, or as an allegorical image of the souls which can either accept or refuse salvation[52].

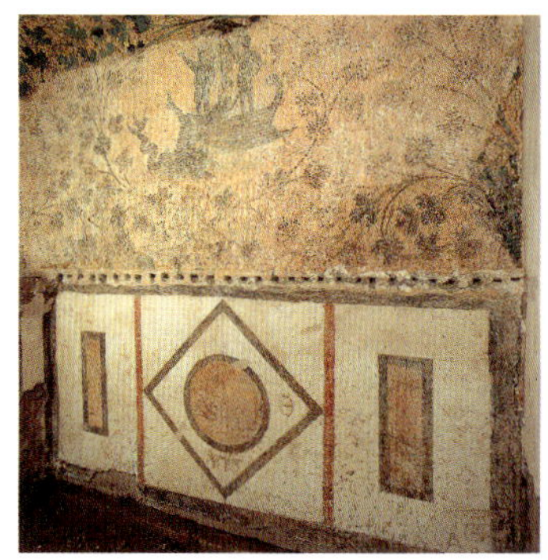

If we are to consider the early 3rd century date usually attributed to this extraordinary iconographic program as correct, then this chamber emerges as the earliest known example of a Christian mosaic cycle. We know that mosaic decorations were occasionally applied to embellish Christian catacomb chambers, as demonstrated by two extant examples from the catacomb of Panfilo, and in the catacomb of Domitilla where we encounter another elaborate iconographic program comprised of Old Testament and New Testament images[53]. Yet these extant examples seem to date at least a century later.

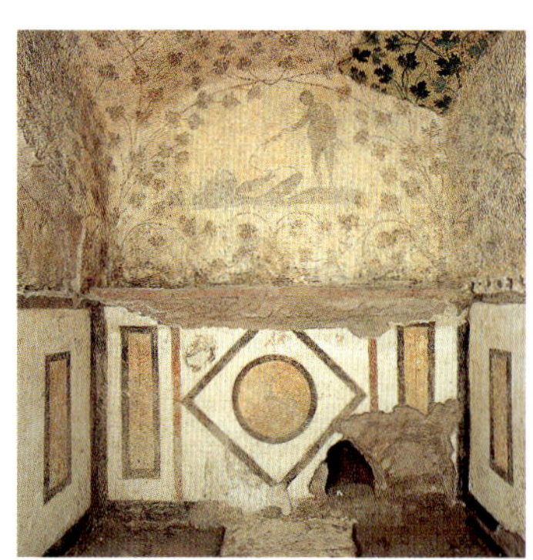

What we encounter then in this extraordinary mausoleum are precious references that can further enlighten our knowledge of how Christian artistic imagery developed in the early centuries. The choice of scenes on the walls are synthetic and simple enough that the transposition from pagan or secular to Christian meaning would have been easily and quickly comprehended. Indeed, as catacomb painting has taught us, the Christian artistic syntax was composed initially of image-signs that communicated to the faithful in a direct way the most basic and fundamental beliefs[54].

The transposition process could become at times more intricate in terms of fusing more than one iconographic source. This is shown by the extraordinary and in many ways unique figure at the center of the vault interpreted as representing Christ - the *sol invictus*, the *sol salutis et iustitiae*. At least two or even three image types have been detected as the sources which have merged to create this iconographic model: the pagan Apollianic (sun-god) image, the emperor's apotheosis scene, and even Ezechial's vision referring to the Ascension of Elijah[55]. All of these individual sources were well known subjects in early Christian art as demonstrated by numerous representations appearing in catacomb painting, ivory dyptics, sarcophagi reliefs.

In the Vatican Mausoleum, the image reveals additional characteristics that strengthen its exceptional iconographic value, as the cross-nimbus (Grabar's analysis of its origin in connection to the Ascension of Elijah scene in Via Latina – p. 117), or the orb held in his left hand that further reveals the influence of imperial imagery tradition[56].

Finally, this central figure, which is also the best preserved, offers to us an example of outstanding technical virtuosity, in the exquisite modelling and attention to naturalistic detail that has been successfully achieved through a chiaroscuro effect applied in areas like Christ's mantle, the depiction of the horses, and the vine leaves. The gold background, the energetic stance of the horses depicted rearing vivaciously, the profile of the mantle undulating vigorously in the air, endows this scene with a momentum, a visionary quality that is swift and transient in character in physical time and space. Yet the same golden background, spelling out a transcendental character, reassures its lasting existence in an heavenly abode.

The message then becomes clear; it is a consoling salvific message of life and hope that transcends all darkness, a message that, for this reason, found in the luminous quality of mosaic craftsmanship its best and ultimate expression.

Notes:

1) Giuseppe Zander, *Antichi Mosaici nella Basilica di San Pietro in Vaticano.* Città del Vaticano: 1985.

2) J.L. Benson, *The Inner Nature of Color.* Steiner Books: 2004, pp. 24-26.

3) Apollo and Daphne group now in the Borghese Gallery, Rome.

4) One of the most exquisite treatments of surface textures is best seen in the sculptural work by Bernini "The ecstasy of Saint Teresa" in S. Maria della Vittoria Church in Rome.

5) See Louis Male.

6) For the date of the first mosaic decoration in the Gregorian chapel, see catalogue of the exhibit in "Collection from the Vatican Mosaic Studio" Knights of Columbus Museum 2001, pp. 8-9.

7) The years of the Pontificate of Leo III: 795 - 816; Zander, pg. 60, plate XXI; G.B. De Rossi, *Mosaici Cristiani delle Chiese di Roma*; described in Codex Barberiniano by Grimaldi in De Rossi; an interesting comparison with similar image in Haghia Sophia Church in Istanbul in John Beckwith Early Christian and Byzantine Art Penguin Books 1979, pp. 190-191.

8) Zander, pp. 62-63, plates XXII, XXIII, XXIV.

9) V. Lanzani, "The Vatican Grottoes" in Revue *«Roma Sacra»*, Elio De Rosa, ed.: 2003, pp. 2-3.

10) Ibid, pp. 7-8.

11) Restrictions particularly strict for women as recorded by Moroni and De Lorbac, see Lanzani, p. 50: in 1841 rules were as follows "In these sacred grottoes women are prohibited to enter, under the pain of excommunication, except on Pentecost Monday when men are prohibited to enter under the same pain. In other times of the year, the pope grants the canons and the major sacristans the faculty to admit women for a visit." (Moroni XI, p. 287).

12) Lanzani, p. 50.

13) See De Rossi.

14) Ibid. who describes the iconographic cycle as follows: above the altar – 7 panels: praying Virgin, pontiff offering model, New Testament scenes – from annunciation to resurrection; left wall – 5 panels representing lives of St. Peter and St. Paul including the martyria; under the tabernacle of the altar – Virgin flanked by the two apostles.

15) Beckwith, p. 154.

16) For a more detailed analysis of the Palimpsest Wall of S. Maria Antiqua Church see E. Kitzinger, *Byzantine Art in the Making.* Harvard University Press: 1980, p. 114.

17) Ibid.

18) Beckwith, p. 151.

19) A. Grabar, *Christian Iconography – A Study of its Origins.* Princeton University Press: 1968, p. 74; Zander, plate IV, p. 20; Lanzani, fig. 39.

20) Beckwith, p. 164, fig. 141.

21) Ibid, p. 151; Zander, plates I, II, III, p. 14-19; De Rossi, plates 1e, 1g, 1c.

22) Beckwith, pp. 26-27.

23) R. Krautheimer, *Early Christian and Byzantine Architecture* .... 1979, p. 60.

24) Ibid, p. 55.

25) For a comparison with Pola casket, see Beckwith, p. 26.

26) Ibid.

27) Lanzani, p. 7, fig. 9.

28) Ibid, p. 47, fig. 77.

29) Pietro Zander, *The Vatican Necropolis. in Revue "Roma Sacra".* Elio De Rosa ed.: 2002, pp. 4-5.

30) With the exception of the barrel vault of Mausoleum N.

31) P. Zander, p. 10.

32) For the discovery of Mausoleum I, see P. Zander, p. 47; see also M. Guarducci Pietro, *Fondamenta della Chiesa...*, p. 18.

33) Guarducci, p. 18; P. Zander, p. 48, fig. 112.

34) Robert Ling, *Ancient Mosaics.* London: 1998, p. 34, regarding the characteristics of the Roman contribution to the mosaic tradition: "the black and white figure style was the major Italian contribution to the history of ancient mosaics", p. 47.

35) Marble relief from S. Apollinare in Classe Church in Ravenna dated mid 6th century in Beckwith, p. 123, fig. 99.

36) Grabar, p. 52, fig. 154.

37) Kitzinger, p. 19.

38) Inscription reads: Quintus Marcius/Hermes sibi/et Marciae/Thrasonidi/Dignitissimae/Conuigi vibis posuit, in P. Zander, p. 20, figs. 38, 39.

39) P. Zander, p. 18.

40) Ibid, p. 19, fig. 37.

41) Ibid, p. 18, fig. 35; Guarducci, pg. 19.

42) Also known as Mausoleum Z "of the Egyptians" in P. Zander, pp. 16-17.

43) Ling, Ch. 6.

44) P. Zander, p. 21.

45) Ling, p. 101.

46) "House of Neptune and Amphirite" in Ling, p. 103.

47) Dated second half of 1st century, Ibid, p. 103.

48) Dated second quarter 1st century, Ling, p. 102.

49) Known of the Iulii, P. Zander, pp. 50-51.

50) Inscription recorded by Tiberio Alfarano, but now lost, according to P. Zander the text "does not contain any Christian elements and must therefore refer to an earlier use of the building", p. 50.

51) P. Zander, p. 50: "this is the only completely Christian mausoleum in the entire necropolis".

52) Guarducci, p. 19; see also Beckwith, p. 19: "Clement of Alexandria placed additional emphasis on the fisherman who recalls the deliverance of Christians by the Apostles from the Sea of the World and the new birth through baptism. Christ is the Fisher of Souls and the soul represented as a fish is washed and reborn through the waters of baptism into a new divine life of Grace - an idea new to the pagan world."

53) Rediscovered and analyzed in 1960 by Father Ferrua, in *Le Catacombe Cristiane di Roma.* Schnell and Steiner Rome 1998, p. 74.

54) Also referred to the "signitive method" in Kitzinger, p. 23; see also Grabar, p. 9.

55) Beckwith, p. 19, fig. 1; Grabar, pp. 116-118, fig. 285.

56) Grabar, p. 117.

"The Vatican Mosaic Studio: The Decoration of St. Peter's Basilica,"

By Dr. Paolo Di Buono, Director, Vatican Mosaic Studio

The illustrious history of the Vatican Mosaic Studio, begun in the 16th century during the pontificate of Gregory XIII Boncompagni (1572-1585) is tied to the history of the Vatican Basilica.

In order to begin the decoration of the new St. Peter's, the pope summoned to Rome expert mosaic artists from Venice who established the first stable team of Roman mosaic artists by teaching their technique to local students. Enamels produced in Venice were used for this initial work.

The dome of the Gregorian Chapel was the first to be decorated between 1578-80, according to cartoons designed by Girolamo Muziano. The results of the decoration were so good that they decided to decorate Michelangelo's dome using mosaic technique.

In order to fix the mosaics onto the wall they introduced for the first time a new technique: a special stucco made with linseed oil. Since this stucco dried slowly, it allowed an easier work pace (the recipe has been jealously kept for over four centuries and is still used today by Studio artists).

From 1598 to 1599, mosaic artists began to work on the pendentives of the major dome with the representations of the four Evangelists following Giovanni de Vecchi and Cesare Nebbia's cartoons. Between 1601 and 1602, Pomarancio made the cartoons for the Clementine Chapel which were then translated in mosaic technique. Finally Pope Clement VIII commissioned Cavalier d'Arpino to design the cartoons for the main dome of the chapel which was decorated in mosaic between 1603 and 1612.

The iconographic program included the glory in the lantern area above depicting angels holding the instruments of the Passion, and representations of Bishops and Patriarchs, the Apostolic college with Christ, the Virgin, and St. John the Baptist in the lunettes below. Giovanni Lanfranco, Andrea Sacchi and Francesco Romanelli made the cartoons for the side domes, which were then executed in mosaic technique by Giovanni Battista Calandra and Guido Ubaldo Abbatini. Abbatini also made the mosaics for the domes of the Holy Sacrament and St. Sebastian chapels, following the cartoons designed by Pietro da Cortona. Abbatini was later replaced in 1656 by Fabio Cristofari, who executed the mosaic decoration of the Pietà chapel. During this

same period the team of mosaic artists worked in the area of St. Gregory's Ottagono. From 1683 to 1727 Cristofari started the transposition of the cartoons designed by Maratta in mosaic technique for the dome of the Presentation Chapel under G. Chiari's direction. The decoration of the chapel in the choir area was executed between 1699 and 1723 by several artists - Ciro Ferri, Maratta himself, Marcantonio Franceschini, Niccolo Ricciolini. The last chapel to be decorated in this period (1724-1746) was the chapel in the Baptistry. Francesco Trevisani designed the cartoons and Pietro Paolo Cristofari directed their execution. In 1727 Pope Benedict XIII decided to raise the mosaic "laboratory" to a permanent department named as the Vatican Mosaic Studio.

By the first half the 18th century the decoration of the chapels inside the Basilica was completed and the transposition in mosaic form of the altarpieces was begun. The reason behind this new project was to prevent the deterioration of the canvases caused by humidity. The first experiment had begun in the 17th century when Giovanni Battista Calandra translated the painting of St. Michael the Archangel by Cavalier d'Arpino in mosaic form for the synonymous Chapel. The work was considered satisfactory at the time but it was not extended to the other chapels. In order to obtain a greater variety of colors for the altarpieces a furnace was built in 1731 inside the Vatican. By experimenting with new mixtures a great amount of different enamel hues were produced (a part of which are still kept in the Studio's storage rooms). The furnace worker Alessio Mattioli was able to produce a great quantity of colors for skin tones. This technical perfectionism in enamel production made mosaics look like paintings. Many of these recipes are still used today thanks to the inventories preserved in the Historical Archives of the Fabbrica of St. Peter.

Filament Mosaic

The 18th century represents for mosaics production in general and for the Mosaic Studio a period of experimentation. Around 1775 Giacomo Raffaelli invented the filament enamel technique which was employed to make the first "miniature" mosaics or "micromosaics".

The enamels are heated with a flame and are then modeled and pulled with metal tweezers in order to create rods of which sections are cut off to form tesserae.

The invention of this method introduced a new era in mosaic production which now can become so minute to decorate small objects used in daily life like jewelry and tobacco boxes, jewels, etc. that were particularly commissioned by the aristocracy of the "Grand Tour". By the end of the 18th century the so-called "small mosaics" representing secular subjects were introduced as part of the Vatican Mosaic Studio's production giving it international fame. The Studio's craftsmen became the able interpreters of this technique, so much so that the popes would commission them to execute precious gifts for European sovereigns, like the famous table with Achilles' shield that Pope Leo XIII donated to the King of France Charles X in 1826 now conserved at Grand Trianon.

The Mosaic School in the XIX and the XX century

The French occupation of Rome in the 19th century had an important influence on the Vatican Studio's activity. It was moved from the Foundry Santa Marta - which was humid and unhealthy - to the Palace of the Sant'Uffizio, where it remained during the entire occupation period. The imperial administration endorsed the Mosaic Studio, promoting and encouraging its activity to the point of establishing a branch in Paris - The Ecole Imperiale des Mosaiques. When the pontifical government returned the Studio was moved to the Giraud Palace in Scossacavalli, an area of the Borgo where it remained for a short time until 1825 when it was moved again to the Apostolic Palace in the Gallery area near the San Damaso courtyard.

During the 19th century the Studio was busy executing the mosaic decoration of the altarpieces inside St. Peter's Basilica as well as in the restoration - renovation project of St. Paul's Basilica outside the Walls that had been devastated by a fire in 1823. It involved the production of 265 medallions with the portraits of the popes and the mosaic cycle in the facade. During the 19th and 20th centuries, the Vatican Studio conducted restoration work in other basilicas and restored ancient Roman mosaics discovered during archeological excavations.

In the 20th century, the Studio has concentrated on the production of individual compositions made by filate technique onto metal or marble trays and inspired from famous paintings or mosaic originals with both religious and secular subject matters. During this same century the mosaic decoration of the altarpieces inside St. Peter's Basilica was finally completed with the execution of the altarpiece of St. Joseph - Patron of the Universal Church in 1963 following the cartoons designed by Achille Funi.

By 1931, the Fabbrica of St. Peter had built for the Studio a specific headquarters behind the apse of St. Peter where it remained until 1997 when the building was demolished for the construction of the Vatican parking lot. The Studio was thus moved to the ground floor of the old St. Marta Hospice nearby the Audience Hall of Pope Paul VI and St. Peter's Basilica's Sacristy.

The Vatican Mosaic Studio Today: Artistic Production and Restoration

Today the Vatican Mosaic Studio, supervised by the "Reverenda Fabbrica di San Pietro" conducts a double task: the production of mosaic works intended to be sold to the public and the maintenance as well as protection of the mosaic decoration inside St. Peter's Basilica (with interventions aimed at restoration). Thanks to the mastery and experience of its mosaic artist, the Vatican Mosaic Studio carries out work that is inspired by masterpieces of ancient, medieval, modern and contemporary art. Both mastery and experience benefit from a vast array of chromatic shades of enamels.

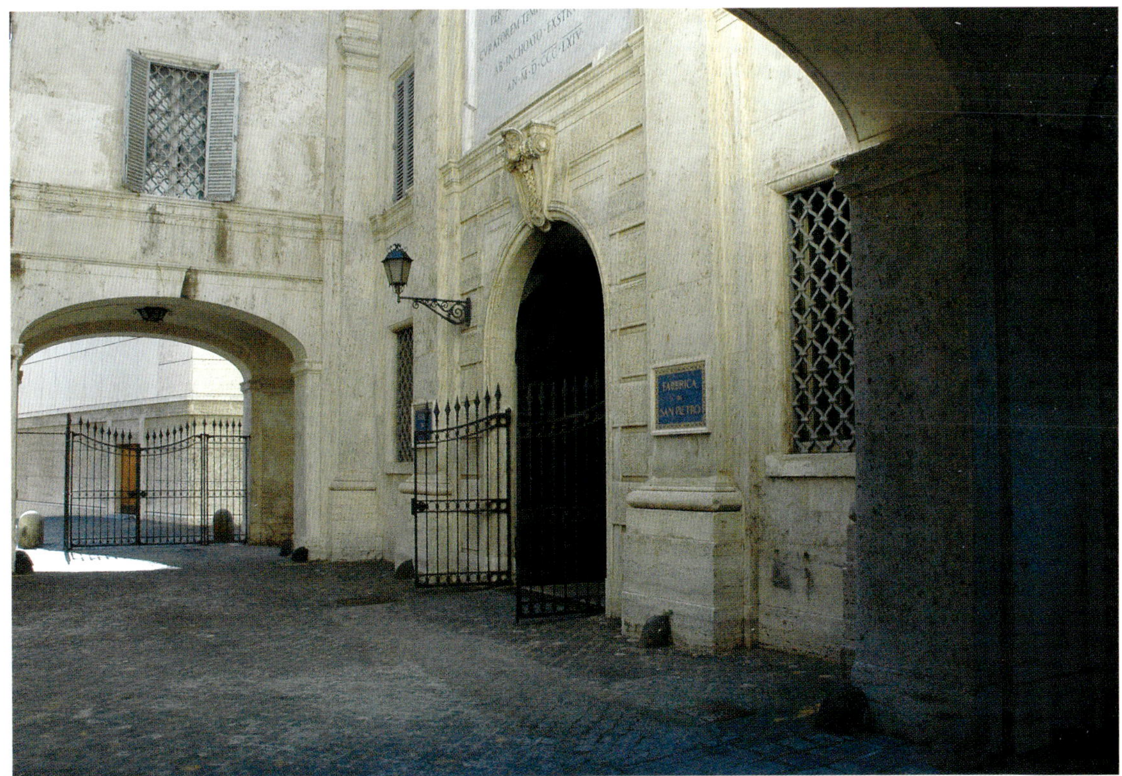

caption, caption, caption, caption, caption, caption, caption

The Vatican Mosaic Studio also executes works on private commission: pictures and also panels are created in its laboratory that can be applied on every kind of surface and in any suitable place.

For the production of its artistic works, the Vatican Mosaic Studio makes use of the traditional techniques "tagliato" (cut natural stones or enamels) and "filato" (filament glass enamel). The latter is more often employed and characterizes the Studio's artistic activity.

Artistic Projection Techniques and Materials: The Cut Technique

The oldest mosaic technique is the cut technique. It precisely consists of cutting the mosaic material (natural stones or enamels) with the help of a special mosaic hammer (martheline) and of a harotic fixed to a wooden log. The material is hit and split into small pieces, thus obtaining, so to speak, the "mosaic basic unit of measurement" or the "tessera".

The difficulty of this procedure varies according to the quality of the material to be cut. As far as natural stones are concerned, it is necessary to follow their physical structure, in order to orientate the cut in the right manner.

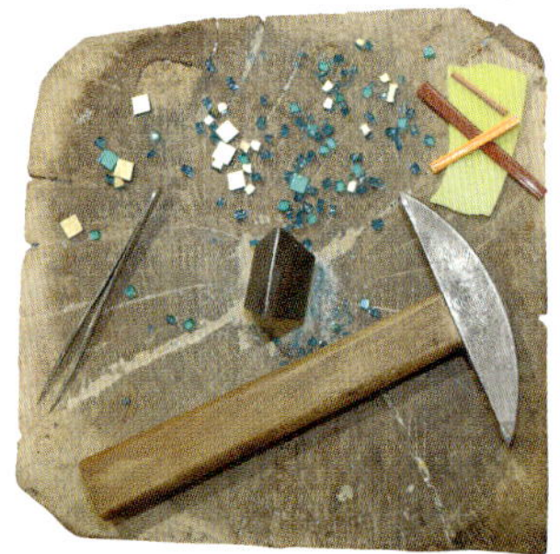

Enamels, instead, have a basic glass composition and their split is generally more complex because it is more difficult to control the direction of the cut. In order to obtain a clean and linear cut, the "tessera" must be held firmly and a single hard stroke must hit the surface. Often, in fact, and in the case of enamels, the cut may result in an irregular detachment.

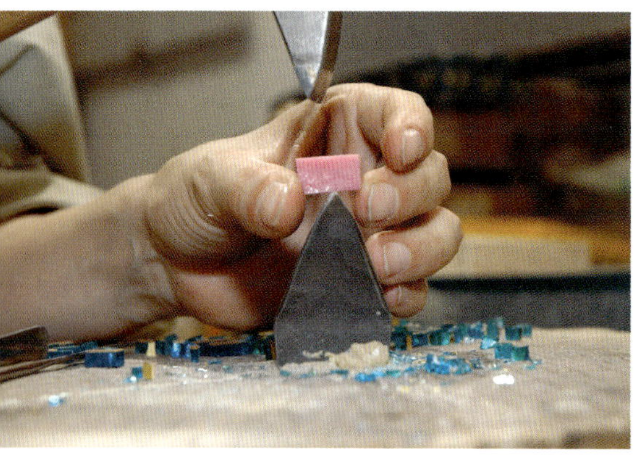

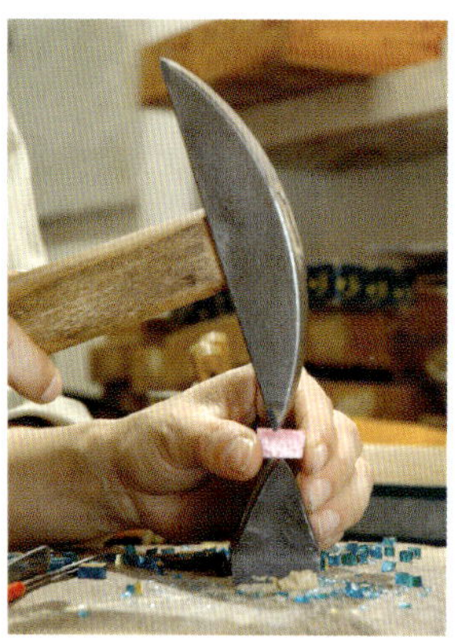

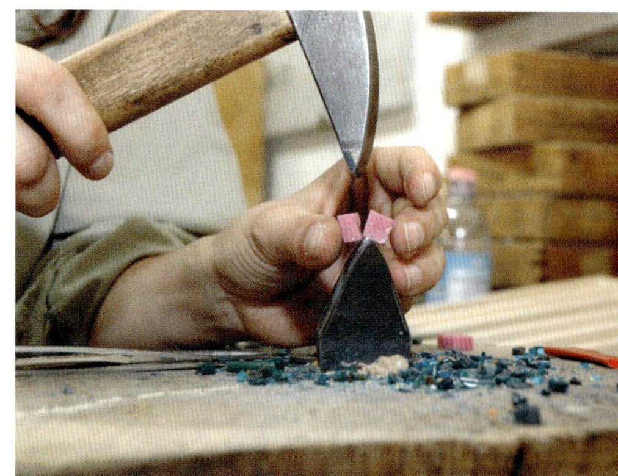

THE MATERIALS

The materials used by the Vatican Mosaic Studio to produce mosaics are natural stones and enamels (vitreous enamels). A wide range of natural stones can be suitable for mosaic decoration. The typology of the natural stones used varies. The major requisite behind the choice of stones - whether they are metamorphic stones (marbles) or sedimentary ones (travertine) - is a compactness and hardness that is suitable to the cut of the hammer and hardie. That is to say they should not be either too hard or too soft. The chromatic range of the natural stones can be rather wide but the color hues are delicate. The enamels have a basic glass composition to which chemical compounds are additionally melted. According to the compound added, one may obtain a specific color.

The creation of enamels, dating back to the Early Middle Ages, begins as an attempt to obtain a greater variety and brightness of colors in comparison to natural stones. The difference in colors of the two materials can be well observed in the photo. Practically speaking, the enamels offer mosaic artists an unlimited chromatic range.

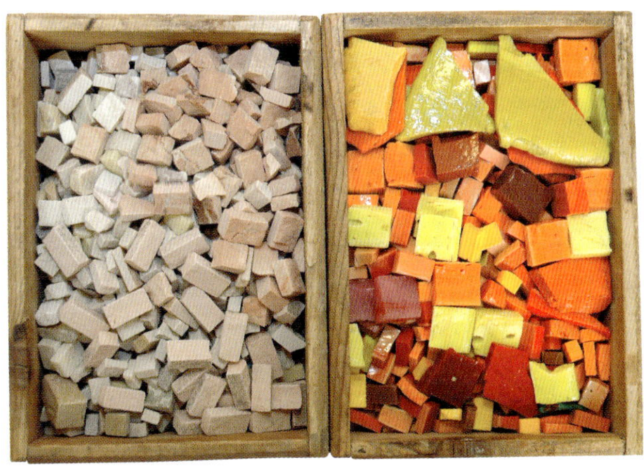

The production technique for enamels is traditionally tied to Venice where, after its arrival from the Byzantine East in medieval times, it was handed down jealously from one generation to another and is still alive today.

THE TECHNIQUE OF FILAMENT MOSAIC

The technique of filament mosaic makes use of vitreous enamels and exploits their characteristic of liquefying at high temperatures. The enamels can therefore be mixed and molded to create rods of different colors and forms. This technique makes mosaic resemble painting as the enamels are mixed as if they were oil or tempera colors until the desired shade is obtained. The difficulty of this technique is due to high temperatures needed for this process.

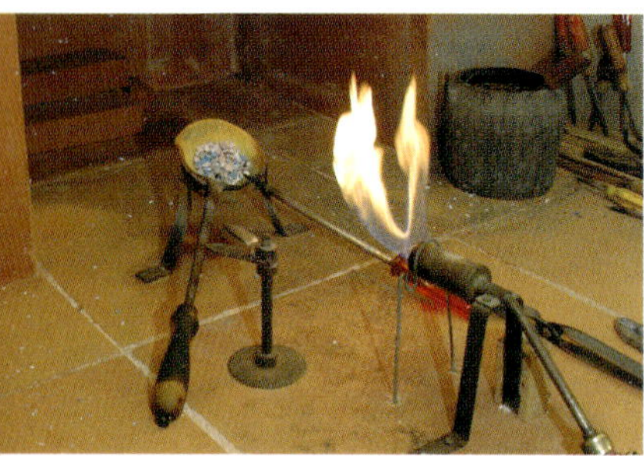
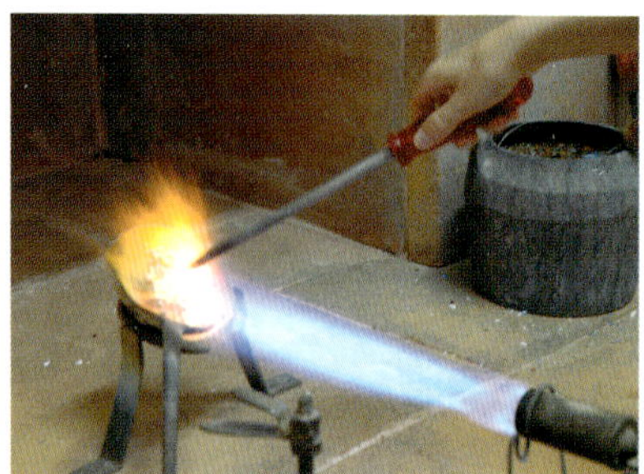
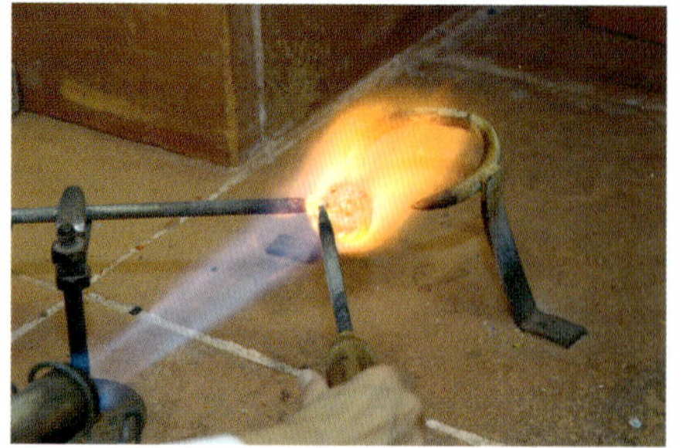

THE PROCEDURE FOLLOWS THE SUBSEQUENT WORK METHOD:

1) The enamels are placed on a hardie towards which a powerful flame generated by gas and air is directed.

2) In the high temperature (about 800-900 C°) the incandescent enamel material becomes viscous and sticky. At that moment it is ready to be detached from the hardie with the help of a metal rod.

3) The heated enamel material is mixed and made compact with the help of the metal rod. By mixing, the air bubbles trapped inside are eliminated.

4) Then with the help of two small marble slabs the incandescent material is molded to the form desired, in this case a rectangle.

5) The enamel material is then pulled with tweezers, to obtain a thin rod. Once cooled, it will become rigid again. The more you pull, the smaller the rod becomes. It is interesting to note that the form given initially to the enamel material is maintained with the same proportions.

In the case of the filament technique, the tesserae are not made with the mosaic hammer and the hardie but from the rods obtained from the spinning procedure. The rods are incised with a sharp file and chipped with tweezers.

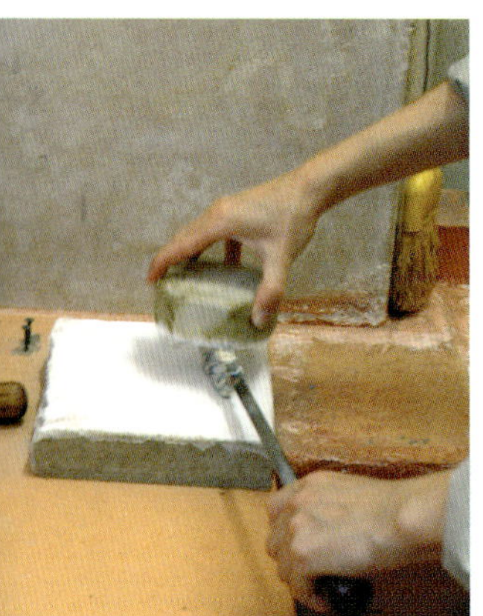
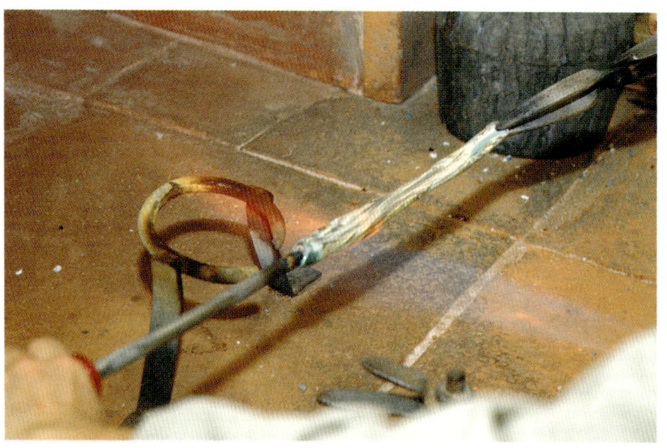
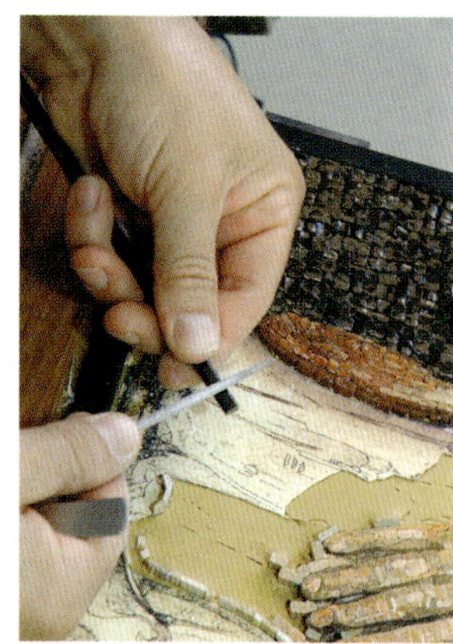

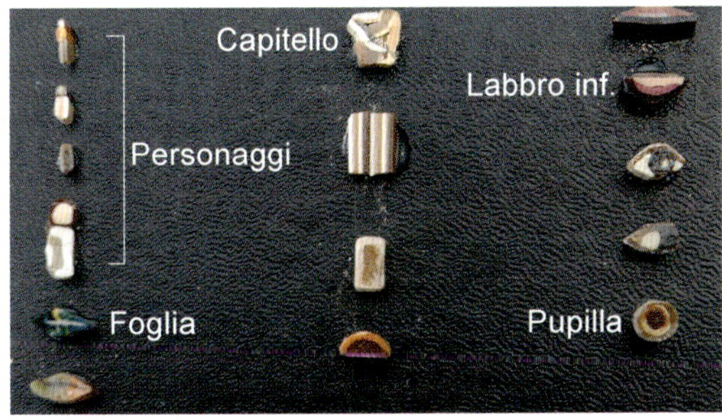

During the melting procedure one can combine two or more colors together in order to form composite hues. This procedure is generally used to simplify the execution of certain features of the composition such as the human figure, the foliage, architectural or anatomical details.

The filament technique enables the production of micromosaics. In fact the more one lengthens the melted enamel material, the smaller the rod's section becomes. This method allows the realization of microscopic tesserae and consequently the production of incredibly minute mosaics.

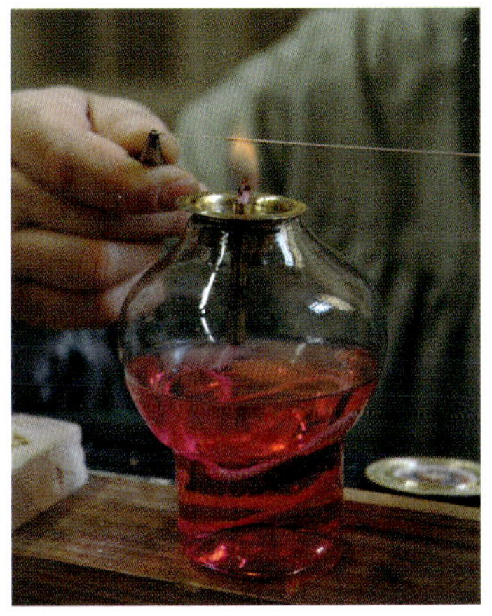

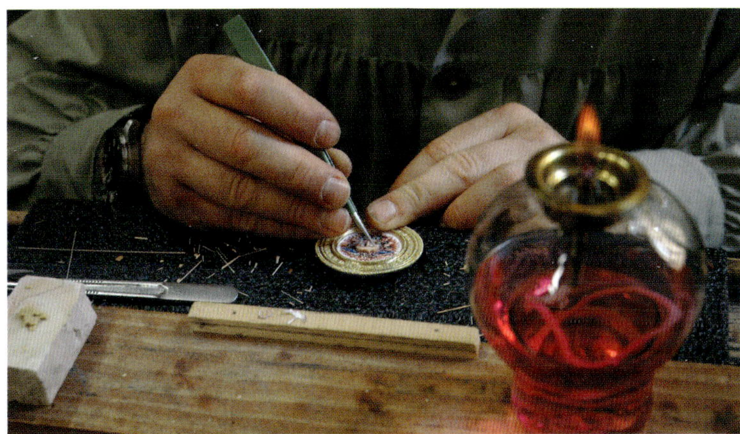

The Phases of Execution of a Mosaic

A layer of stucco (produced by the Studio according to an old and secret recipe handed down from one generation to another) is applied and glued onto a metal support tray outlining the dimensions of the subject one wishes to portray (in this case the Cathedral of Rouen by Monet). A copy of the image to be reproduced is pasted onto the stucco. Using a cutter the image is incised. Once the section of the photo is removed, the tesserae are applied in the stucco portion where the design was impressed. The mosaic is made slowly from the top to the bottom, from left to right as in the writing process.

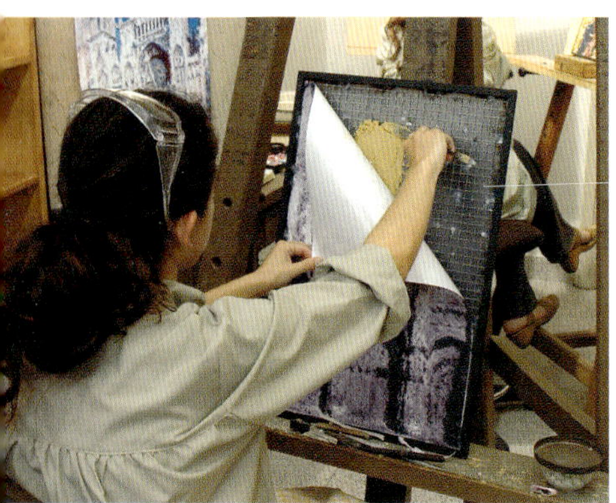

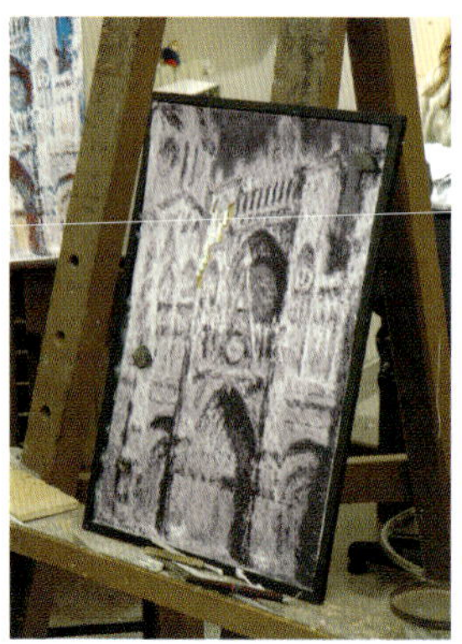

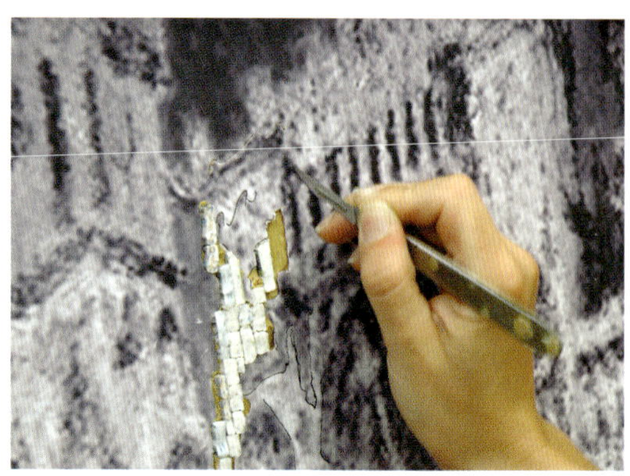

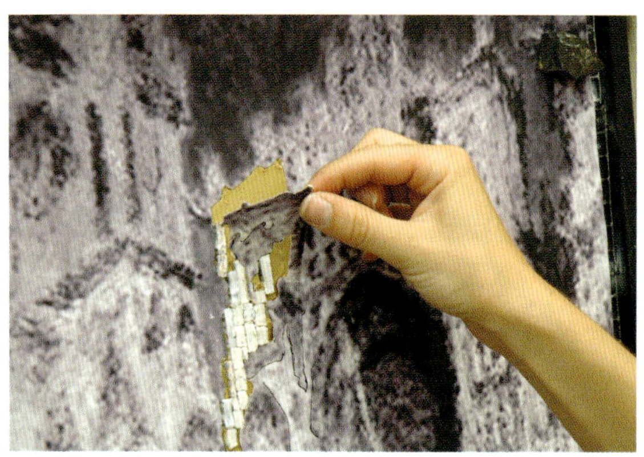

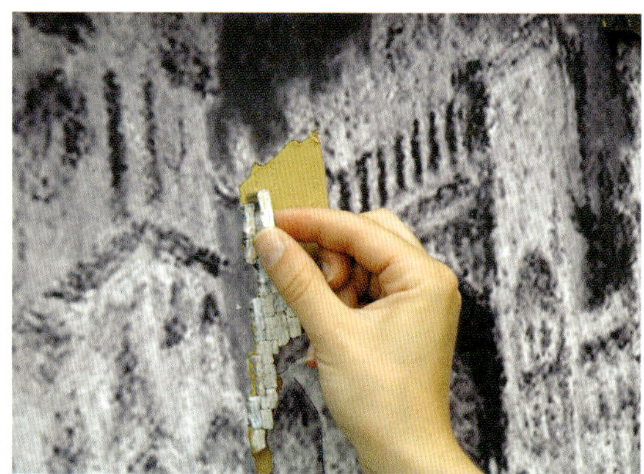

The Restoration of the Dome in the Vestibule of the Chapel of the Presentation in the Vatican Basilica

A restoration campaign was recently conducted (July 2004 - June 2005) on the mosaic decoration of the dome in the vestibule of the Presentation Chapel. Thanks to the support of public and private sponsors, the Fabbrica of St. Peter was able to endow to this important mosaic cycle its original splendor.

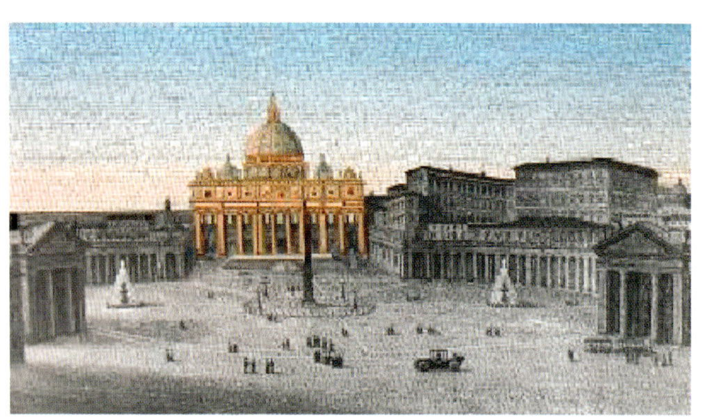

The author of the cartoons for the cupola that inspired the mosaic cycle was Carlo Maratta, one of the most active painters in Rome at the end of the 1600's who was assisted by his disciple Giuseppe Chiari.

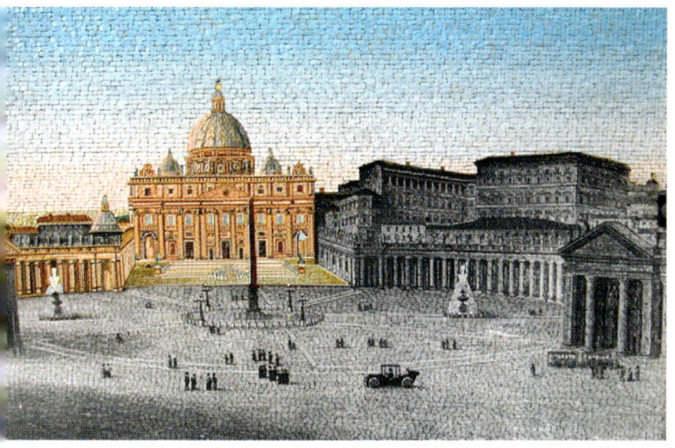

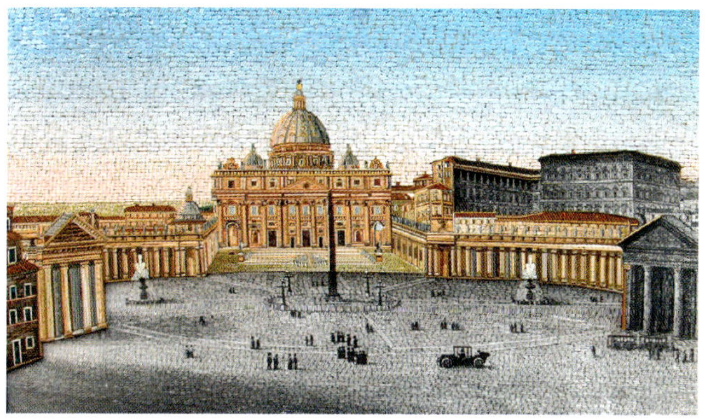

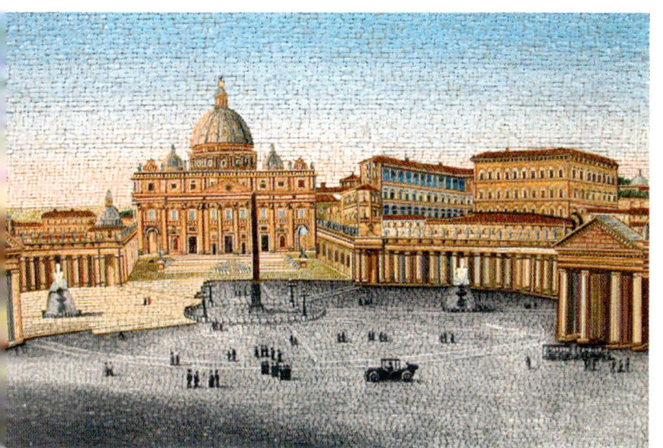

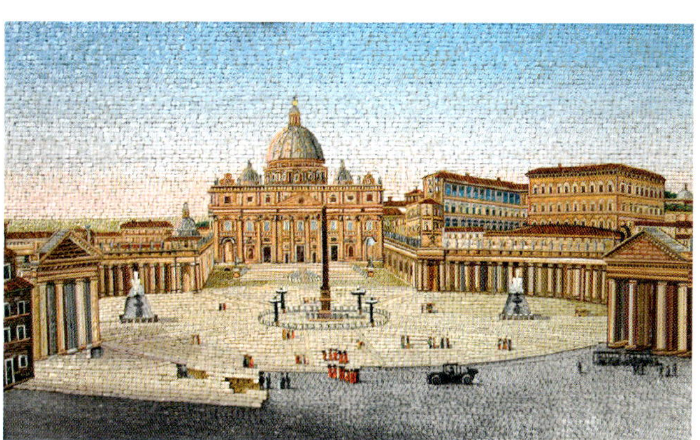

The mosaic cycle, begun in the 1670's, was assigned initially to Fabio Cristofari, a famous artist of the old mosaic school. He was the father of Pietro Paolo Cristofari who founded the Vatican Mosaic Studio.

The work was interrupted in 1689, the year of the mosaic artist's death. The mosaic cycle was finished only in 1725. The other artists who worked on it were: Giuseppe Conti from 1704; Leopoldo del Pozzo from 1717, Domenico Gossoni and Giuseppe Ottaviani. Later Mattia Moretti, Prospero Clori and Mattia de'Rossi also participated.

The iconography focuses on a Marian theme, that includes scenes from the Old Testament depicted in the pendentives and lunettes, the Magnificat in the dome where we find the defeat of Lucifer executed by Chiari and the Coronation of the Queen of Heaven above a choir of angels designed by Maratta. Around the base of the lantern we find the inscription: *RESPEXIT HUMILITATEM - DISPERSIT SUPERBOS* (He has looked upon the humble and dispersed the arrogant) Lk 1,48 and 51. In 1687, Filippo Carcani executed the four stucco angels in the niches around the dome.

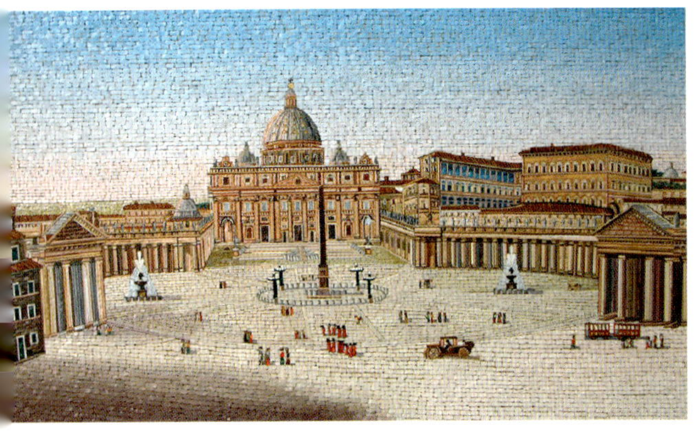
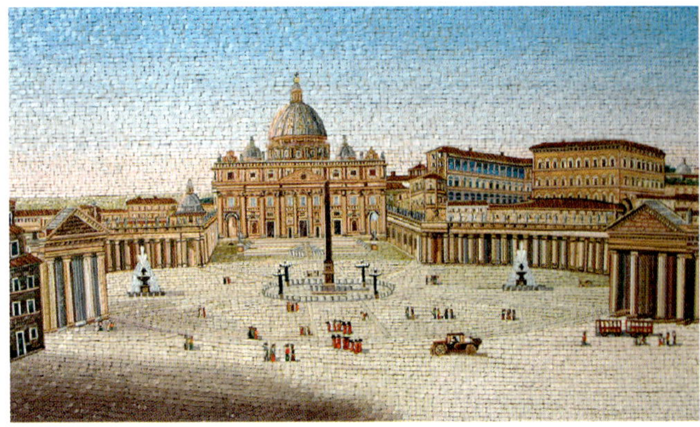

Phases of the restoration

The first operation conducted a basic cleaning of the mosaic surface with water and sponges. The cleaning tests show the different brightness between unclean and clean areas. While the cleaning procedures were conducted, the damaged areas were identified. The second procedure was the marking of the parallels and meridians on the dome surface to create reference axes. During the third phase the figures represented were outlined on tracing paper.

The first area to be restored, since it was the most damaged, was the left hand of the Virgin and her cloak. In the fourth phase, a light fabric called "tarlatana" was pasted to the wall surface using soluble starch glue. The fifth phase consisted in designing the contours of the subjects onto the fabric. The sections of the mosaic designed out on the fabric were numbered. Around the sections where the fabric was applied, in order to protect the areas in a good state of conservation, a series of wood panels were affixed. The entire design of the vault was mapped out on 1:10 scale. The mapping procedure results were useful in the reattachment process of the mosaic portions detached. Next, the deteriorated sections were detached and using the procedure called "spillatura" the deteriorated stucco was removed from them. The following step was the consolidation of the uncovered masonry, removing the remaining stucco and the rusted nails that had been used to attach the mosaic.

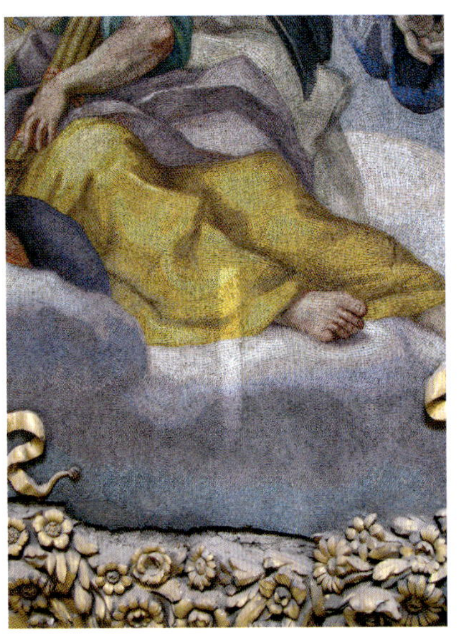

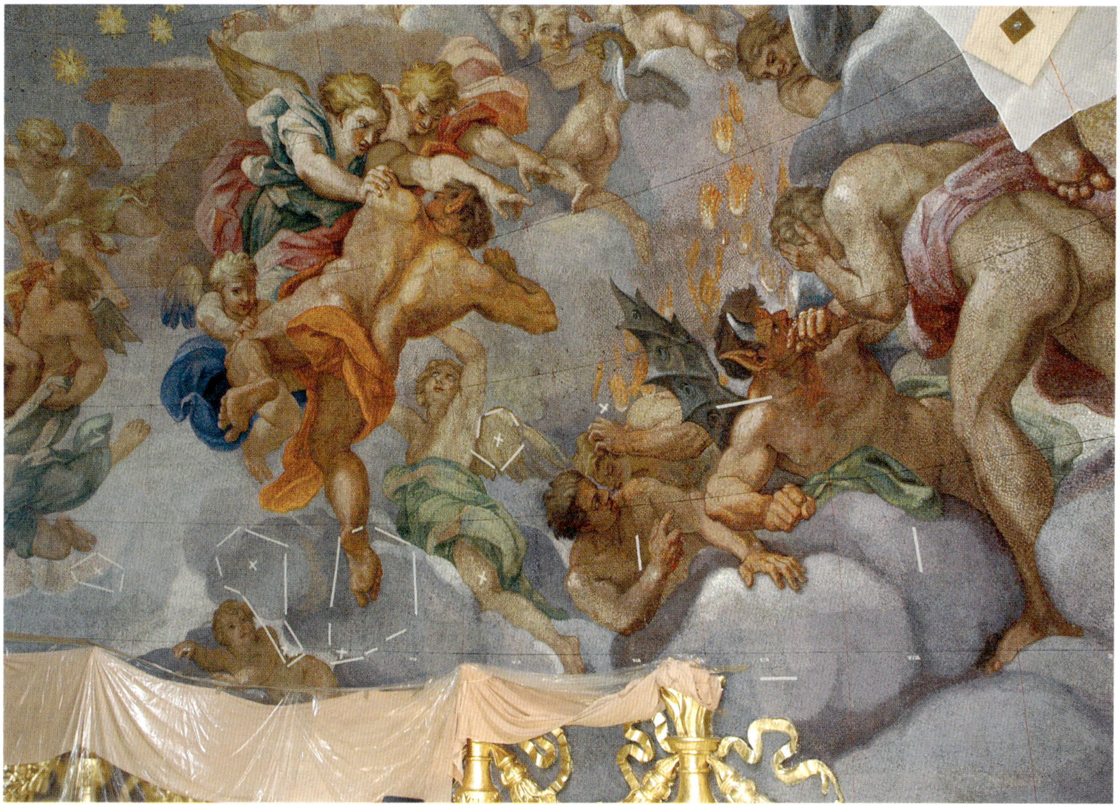

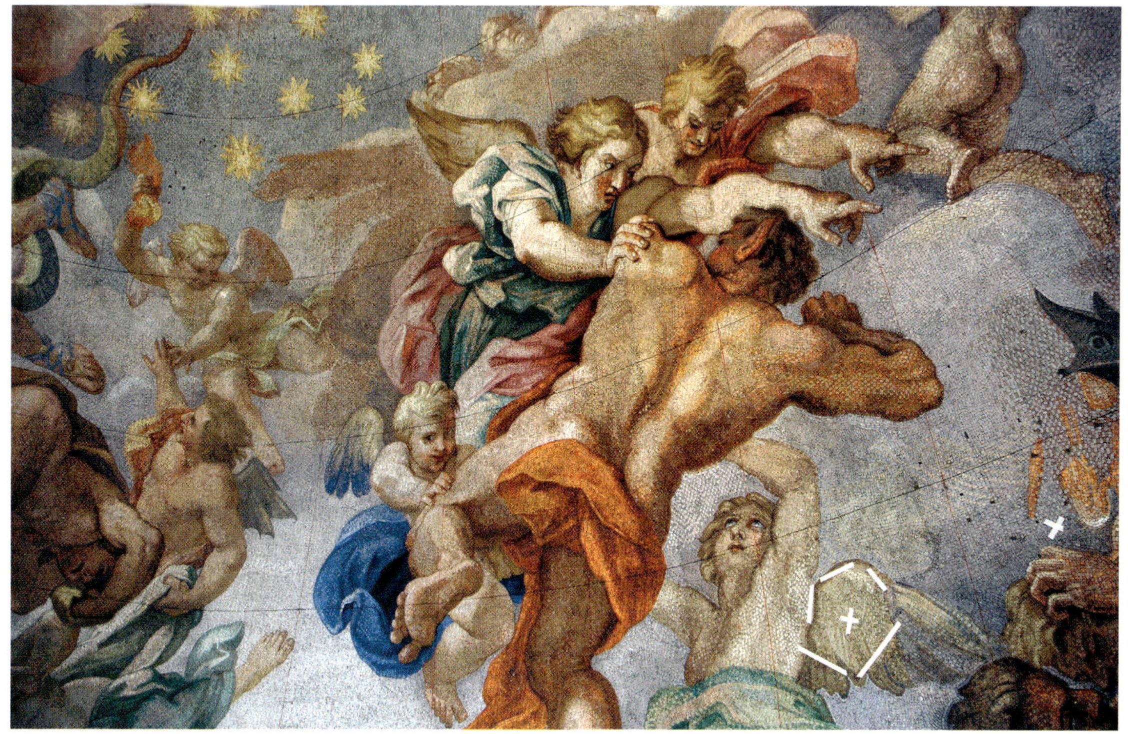

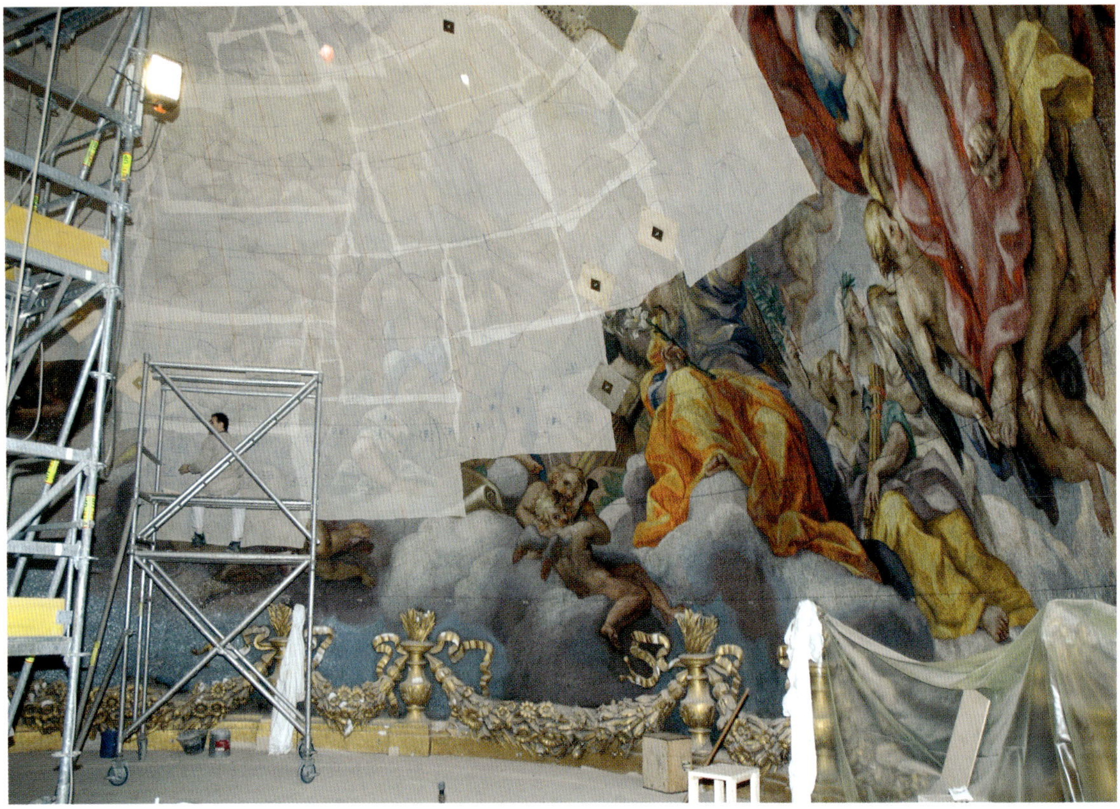

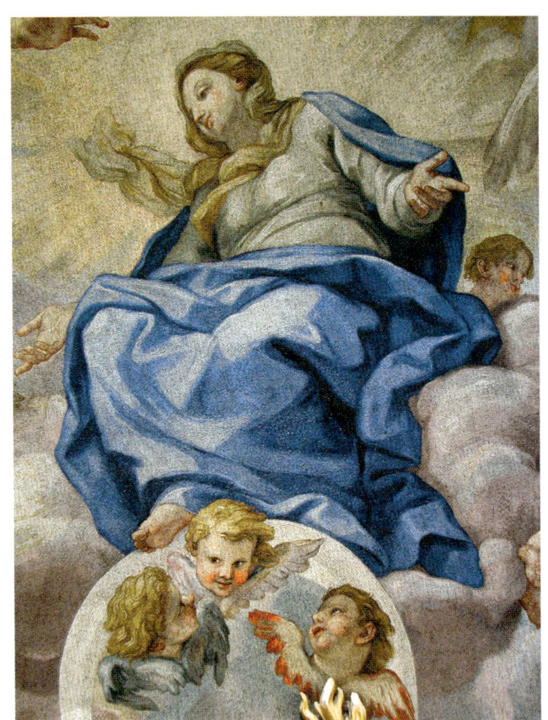

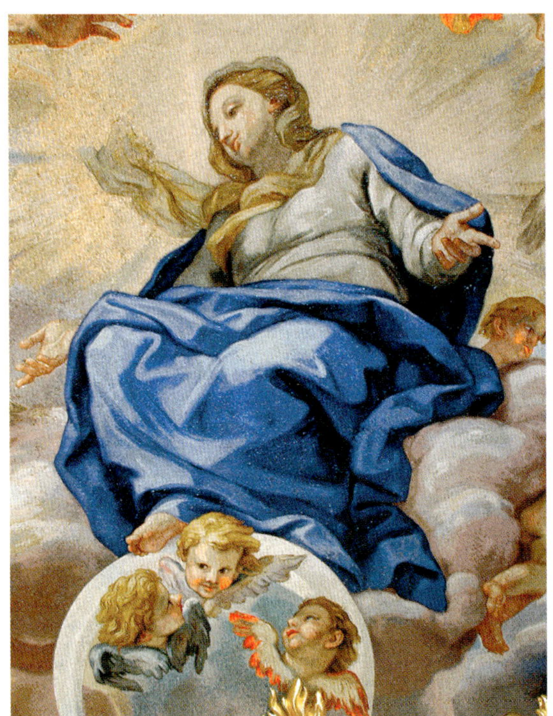

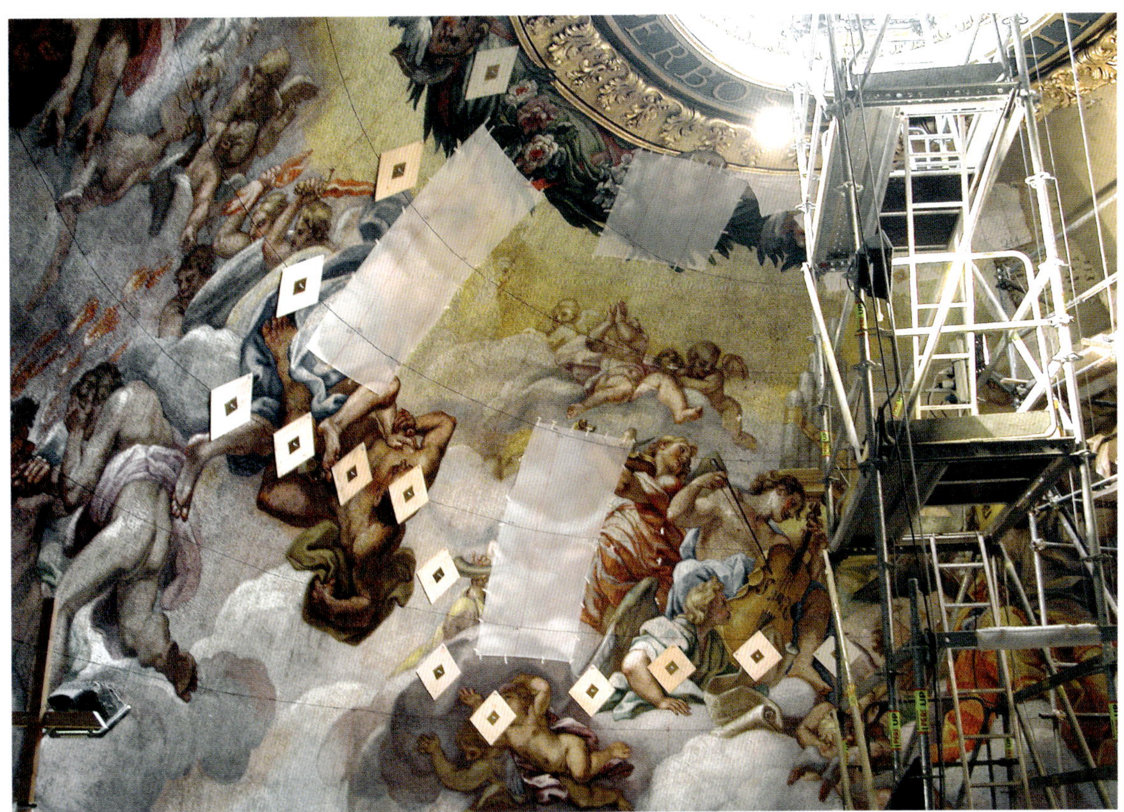

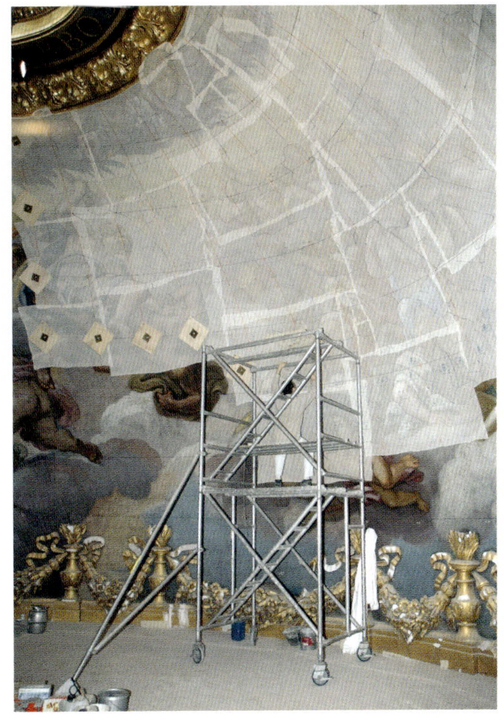

Instead of nails, a stainless steel net was attached with stops, to fix the new stucco to the wall. Then a layer of new plaster was applied. At this point the restored sections of the mosaic were reinserted, according to the mapped out design. After the attachment of two or three sections, the fabric was soaked with water in order to remove it and facilitate the perfect correspondence of the fragments. Finally, the entire interior of the dome was carefully examined to eliminate possible gaps. The cleaning and consolidation procedures concluded the restoration work.

In these recent months, the Fabbrica of St. Peter is organizing a monitoring program in order to evaluate and eventually restore all the mosaic decoration inside St. Peter's Basilica.

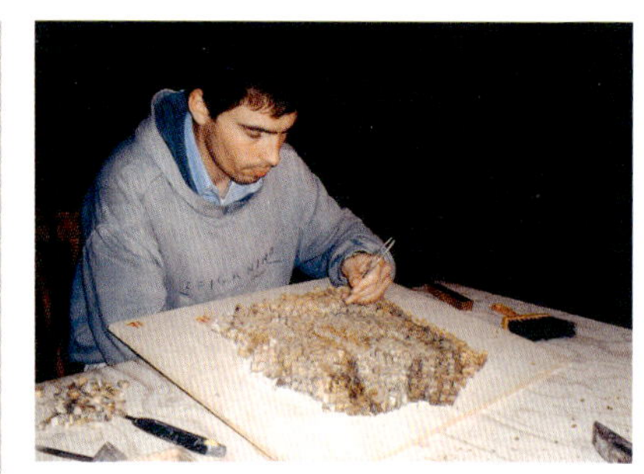
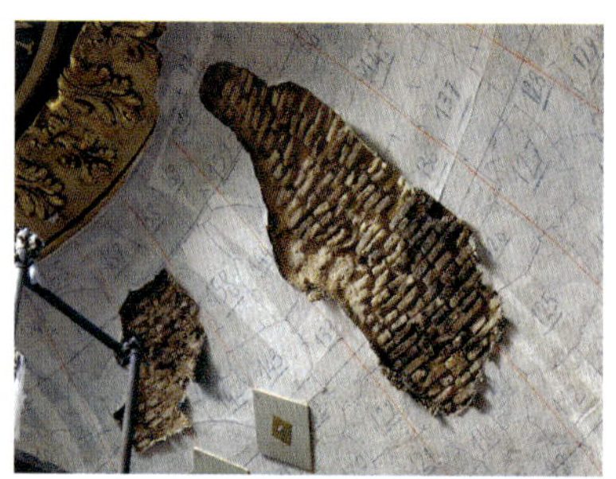
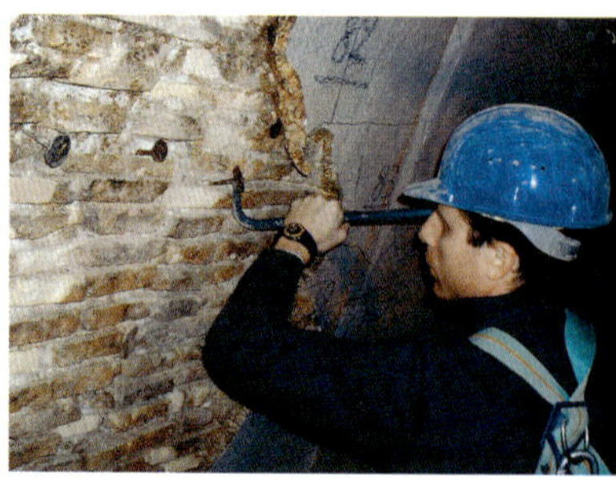
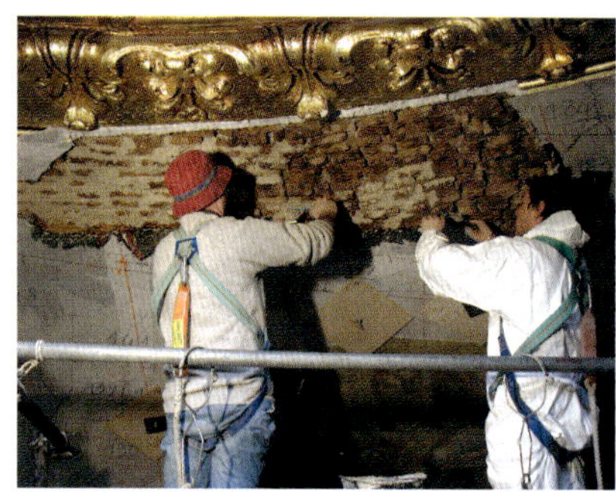
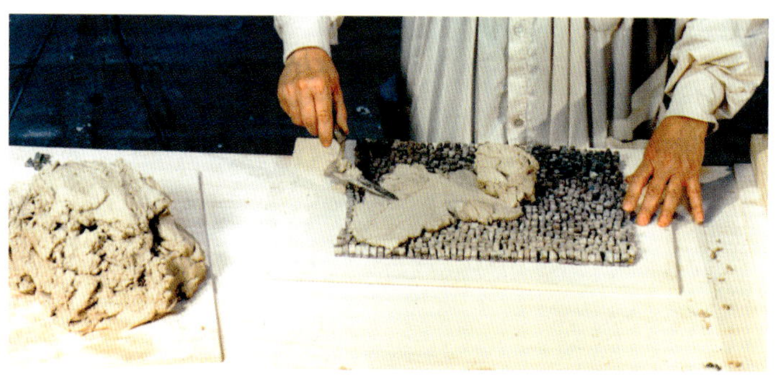
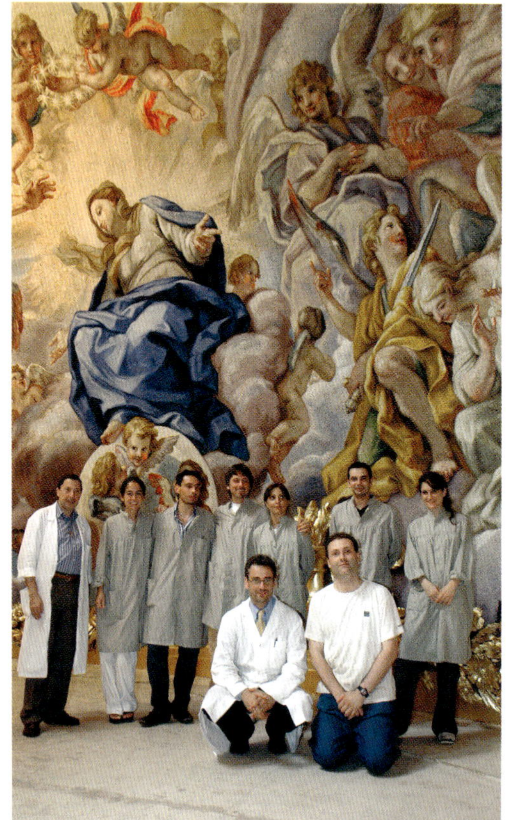
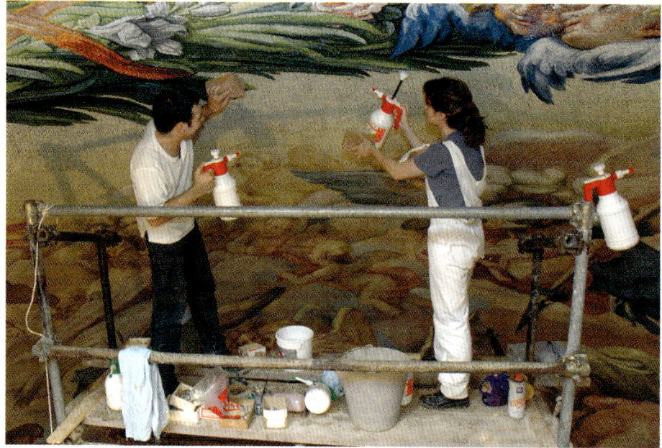
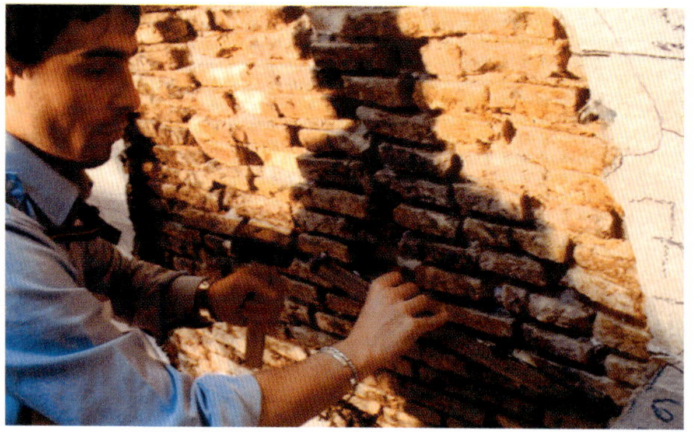

To this day only three of the ten minor cupolas of the Basilica have been restored and this does not include the decoration of Michelangelo's splendid dome.

Considering that the area in question is about 10,000 square meters, one can imagine that it is a long-term project that can be realized only with the support of sponsors who can donate adequate funding.

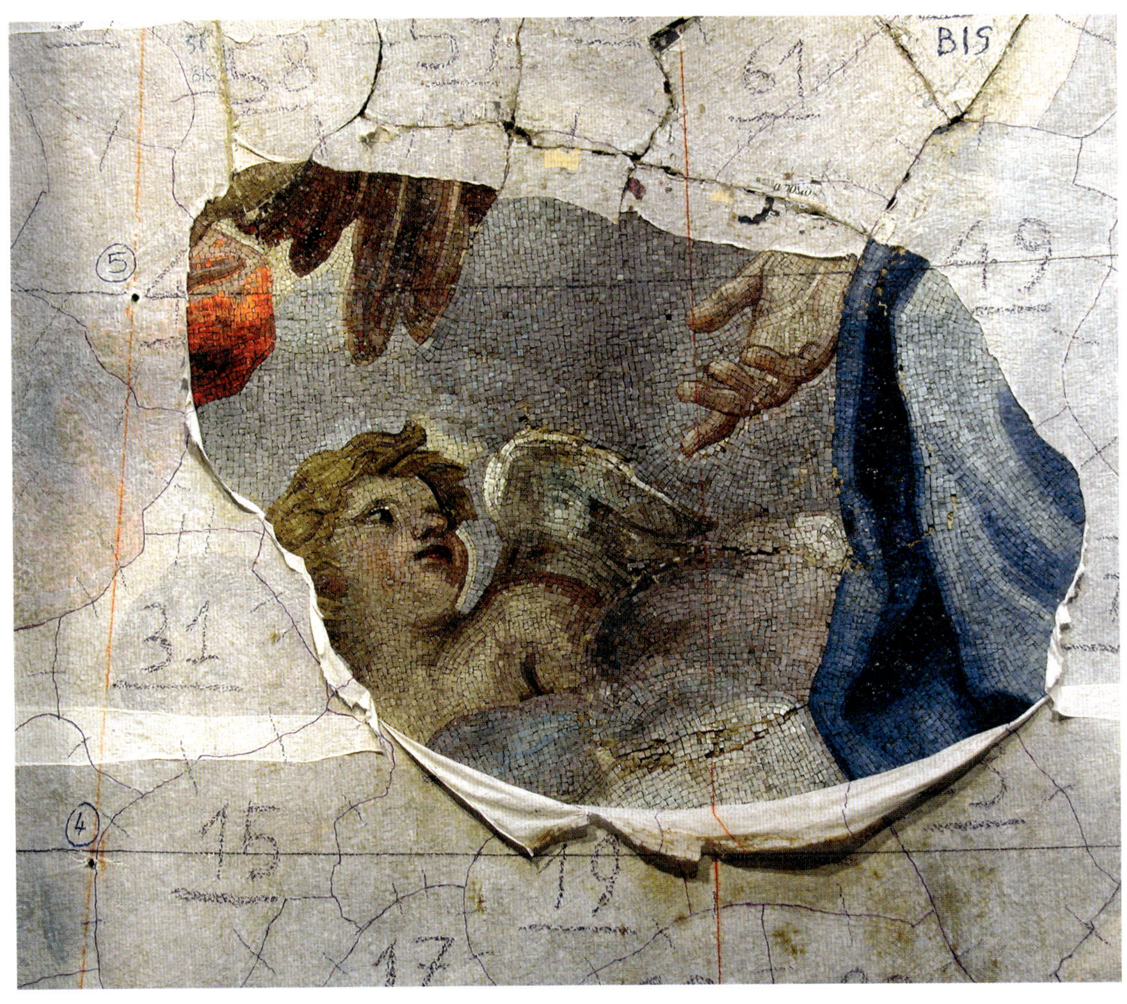

Catalogue of Works on Exibition

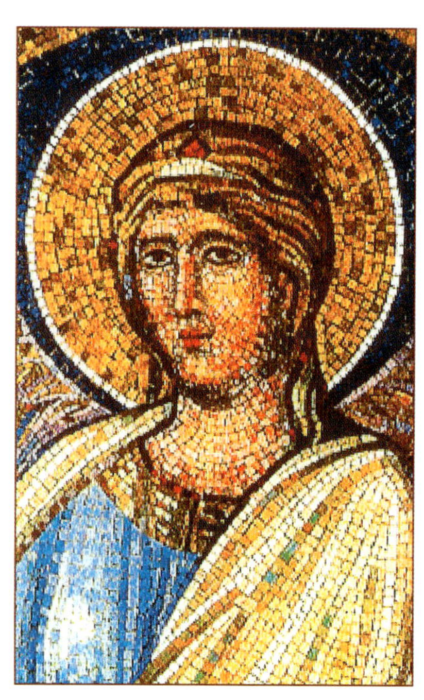

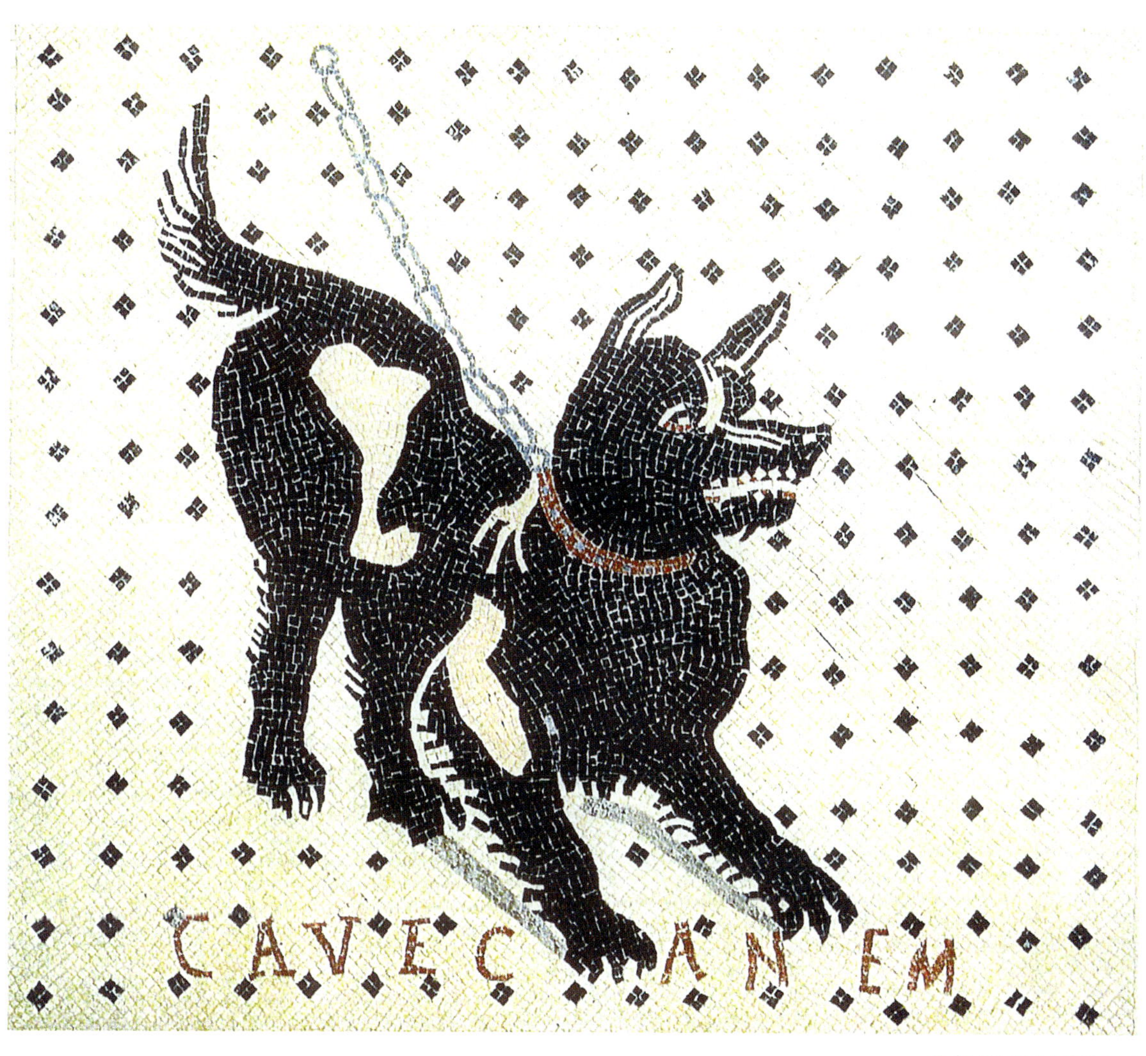

CAVE CANEM

cm. 78x86.
Technique in cut natural stones applied with acrylic resin onto a marble support tray.
Reproduction from an original at "The House of Tragic Poet", 1st century A.D., Pompeia.
Courtesy of Ms. Claudia Huntington and Mr. Marshall Miller.

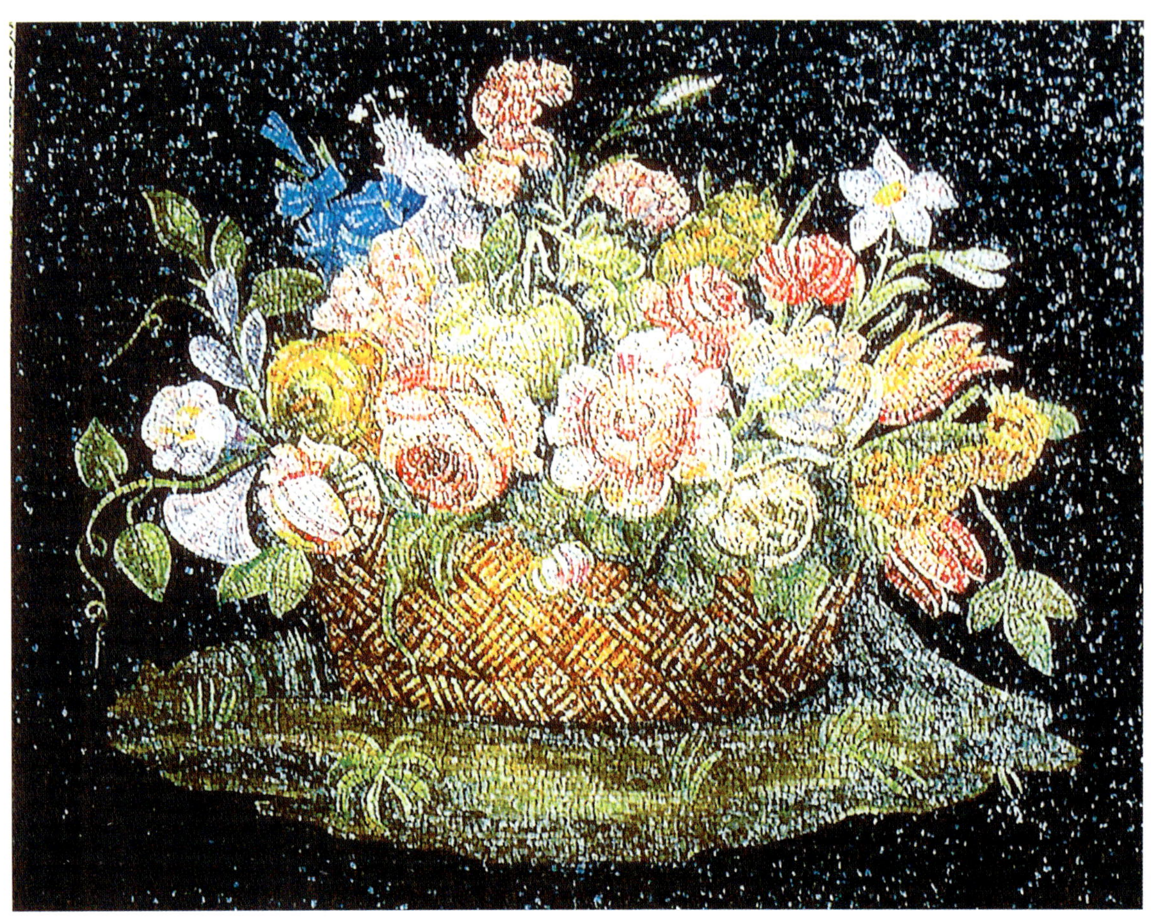

BASKET OF FLOWERS

cm. 74x59.
Cut enamel technique applied with oily stucco onto an iron support tray. Reproduction from a Roman mosaic original, 2nd century A.D.; Vatican Museum collection, Vatican City.
Courtesy of Mr. and Mrs. Wayne Huizenga.

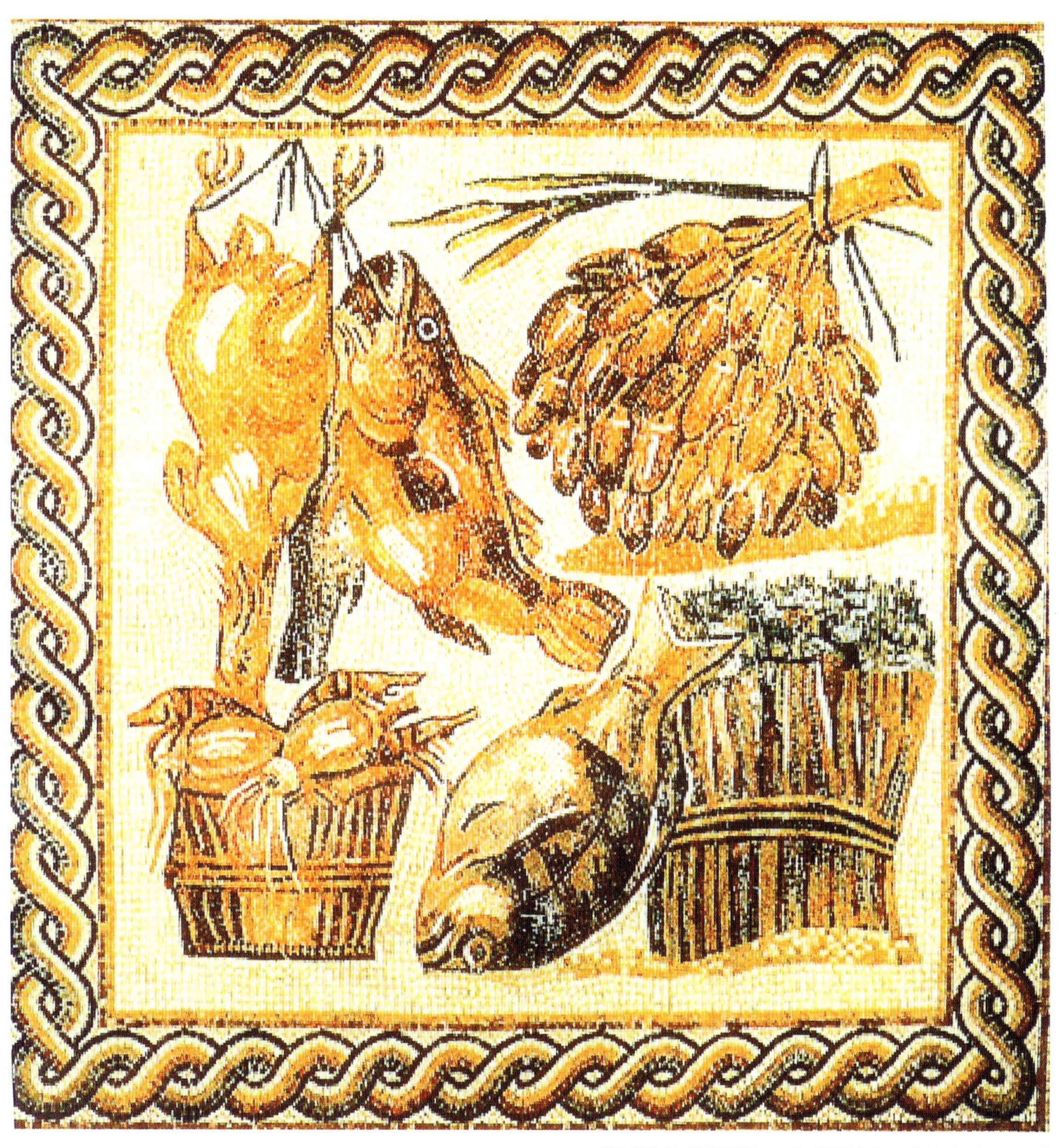

TABLE WITH A ROMAN STILL LIFE

cm. 89x89.
Technique in cut natural stones applied with acrylic resin onto a marble support tray.
Reproduction from a Roman mosaic original, 2nd century A.D.;
Vatican Museum collection, Vatican City.
Courtesy of Ms. Claudia Huntington and Mr. Marshall Miller.

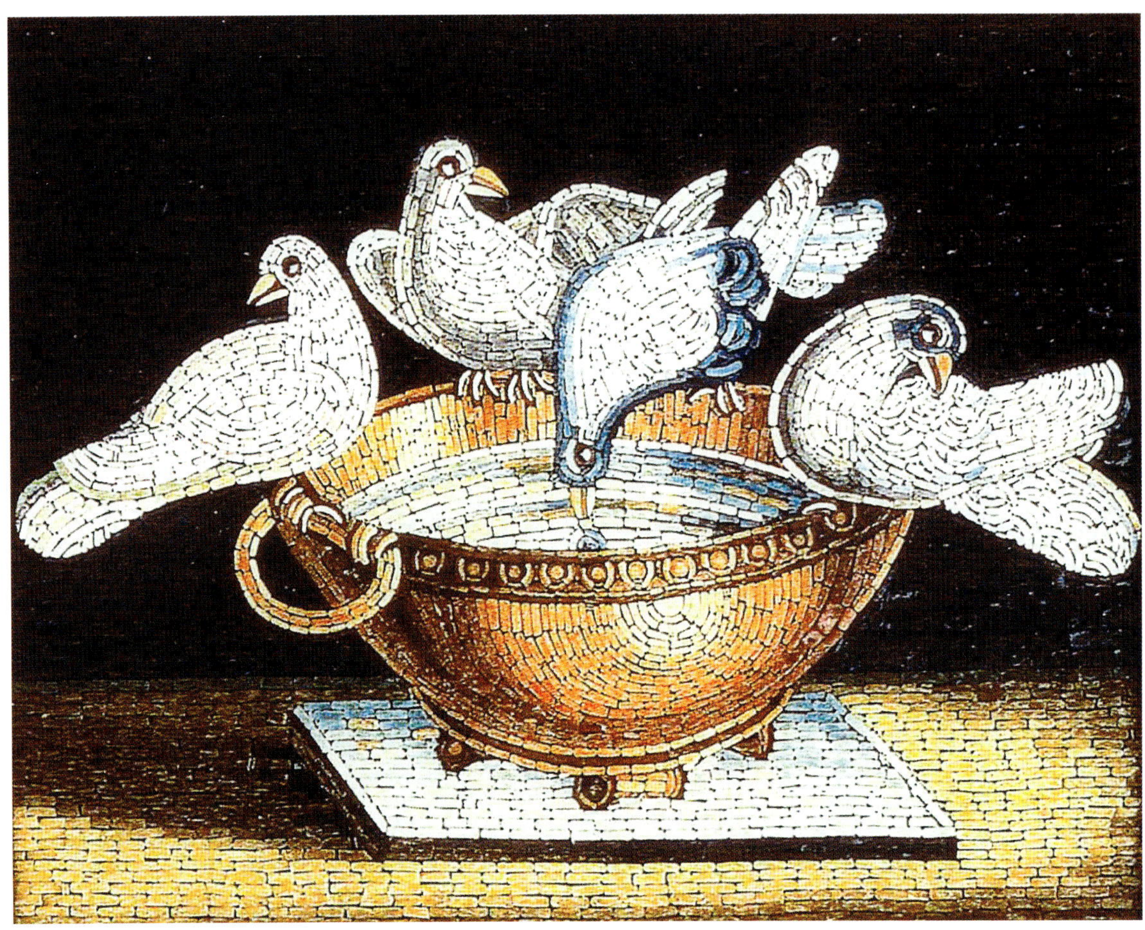

DOVES

cm. 18x14.
Filament enamel technique.
Enamels applied with oily stucco onto an iron support tray.
Reproduction from Roman mosaic original from Hadrian's Villa in Tivoli, attributed to artist Sosos, 2nd century A.D.; Capitoline Museum collection, Rome.

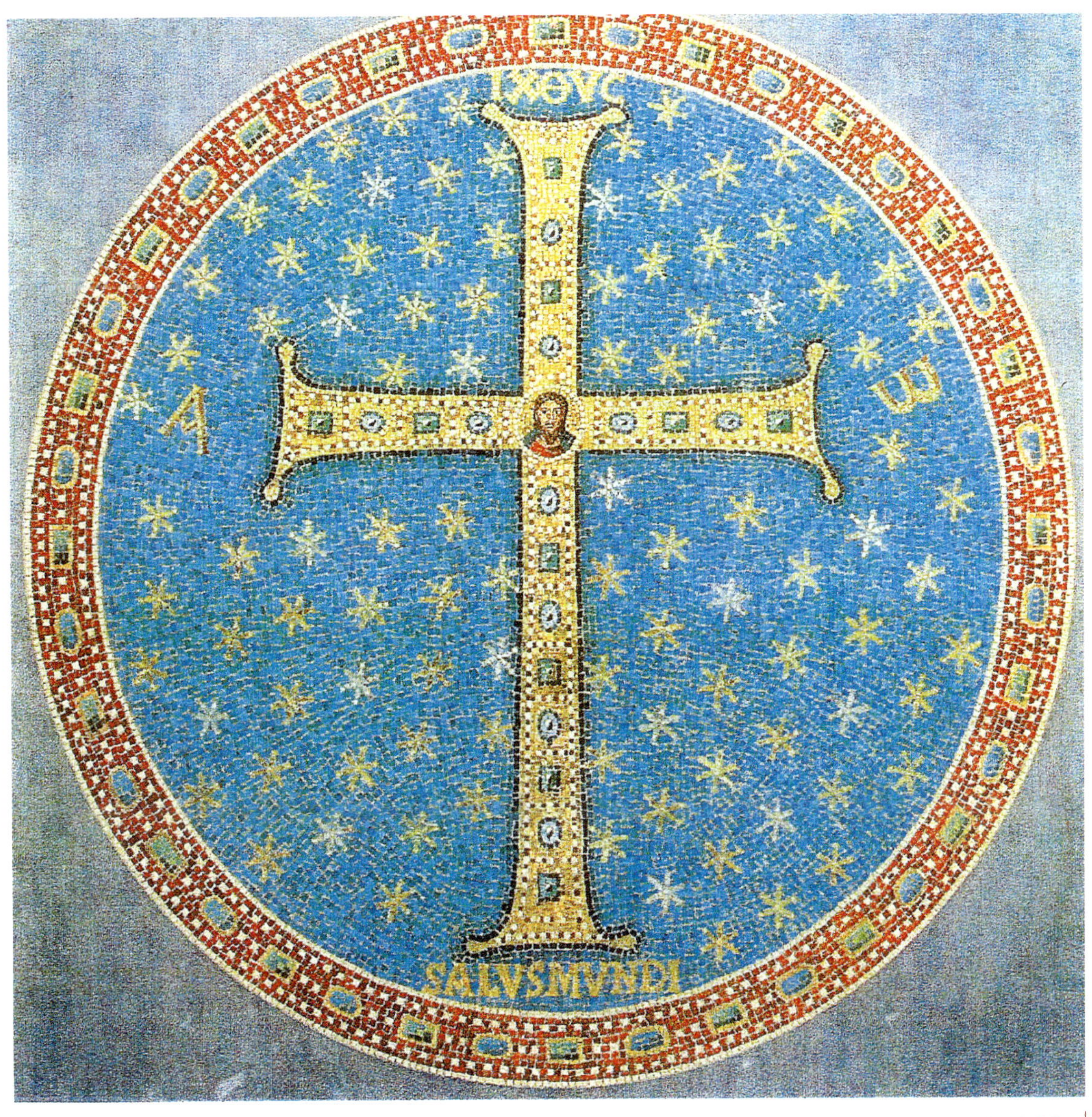

BYZANTINE CROSS

cm. 133x133.
Technique in cut natural stones and enamels applied with acrylic resin onto a marble support tray.
Reproduction from apse mosaic, 6th century A.D.;
St. Apollinare in Classe Basilica, Ravenna.

TABLE WITH NILOTIC SCENES

cm. 175x88.
Technique in cut natural stones applied with acrylic resin onto a marble support tray.
Reproduction from a Roman mosaic original, 2nd century A.D.;
National Archaeological Museum, Naples.

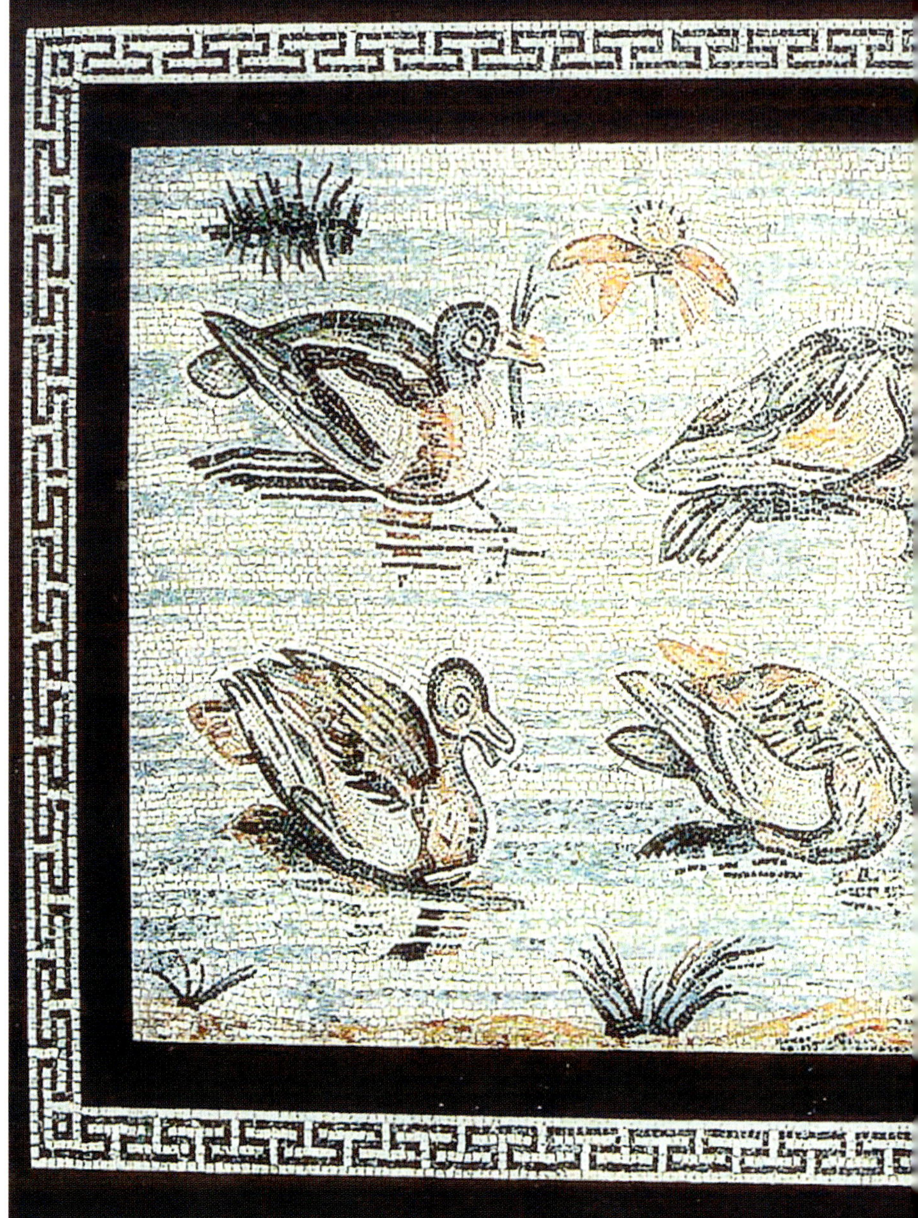

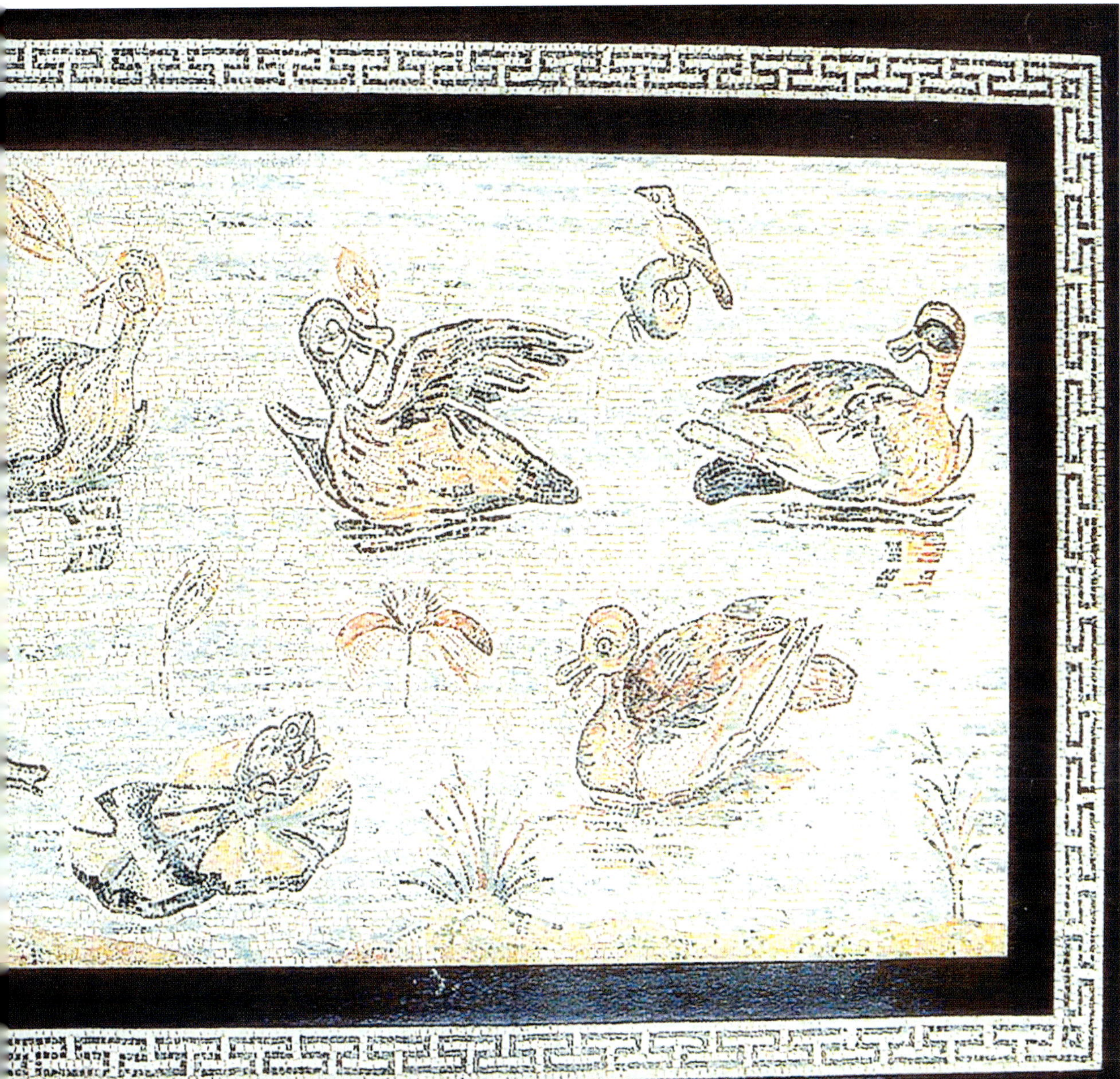

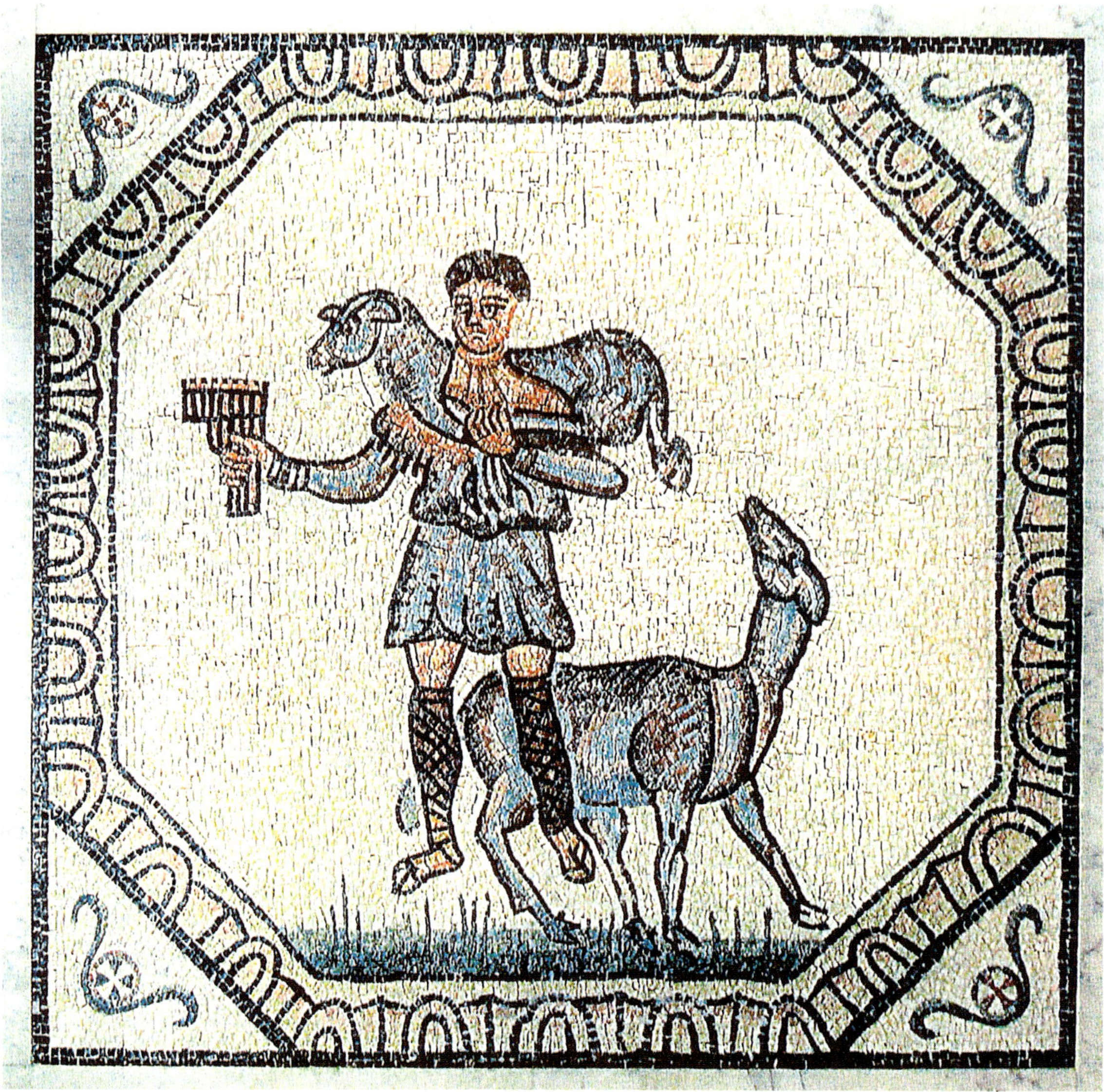

THE GOOD SHEPHERD

cm. 112x106.
Technique in cut natural stones applied with acrylic resin onto a marble support tray.
Reproduction of The Good Shepherd emblem, 4th-5th century A.D.; Early Christian Basilica, Aquileia.

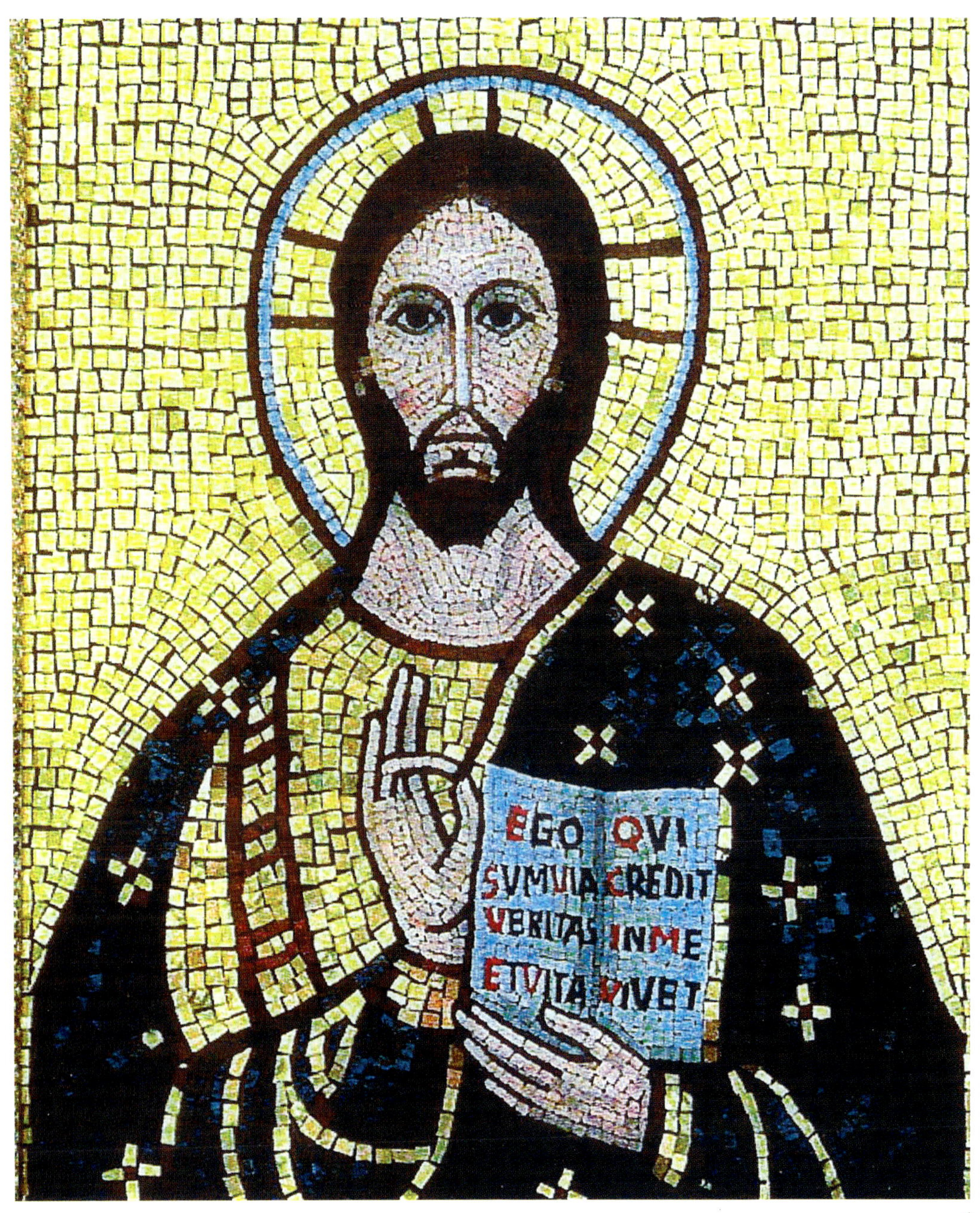

CHRIST PANTOCRATOR

cm. 35x50.
Cut and filament enamel techniques using polychrome enamels and gilt glass fixed onto an iron support tray with oily stucco. Reproduction from the mosaic panel in Nicchia dei Pallii, 8th-9th century A.D.; St. Peter's Basilica, Vatican City.
Courtesy of Mr. and Mrs. Thomas Monaghan.

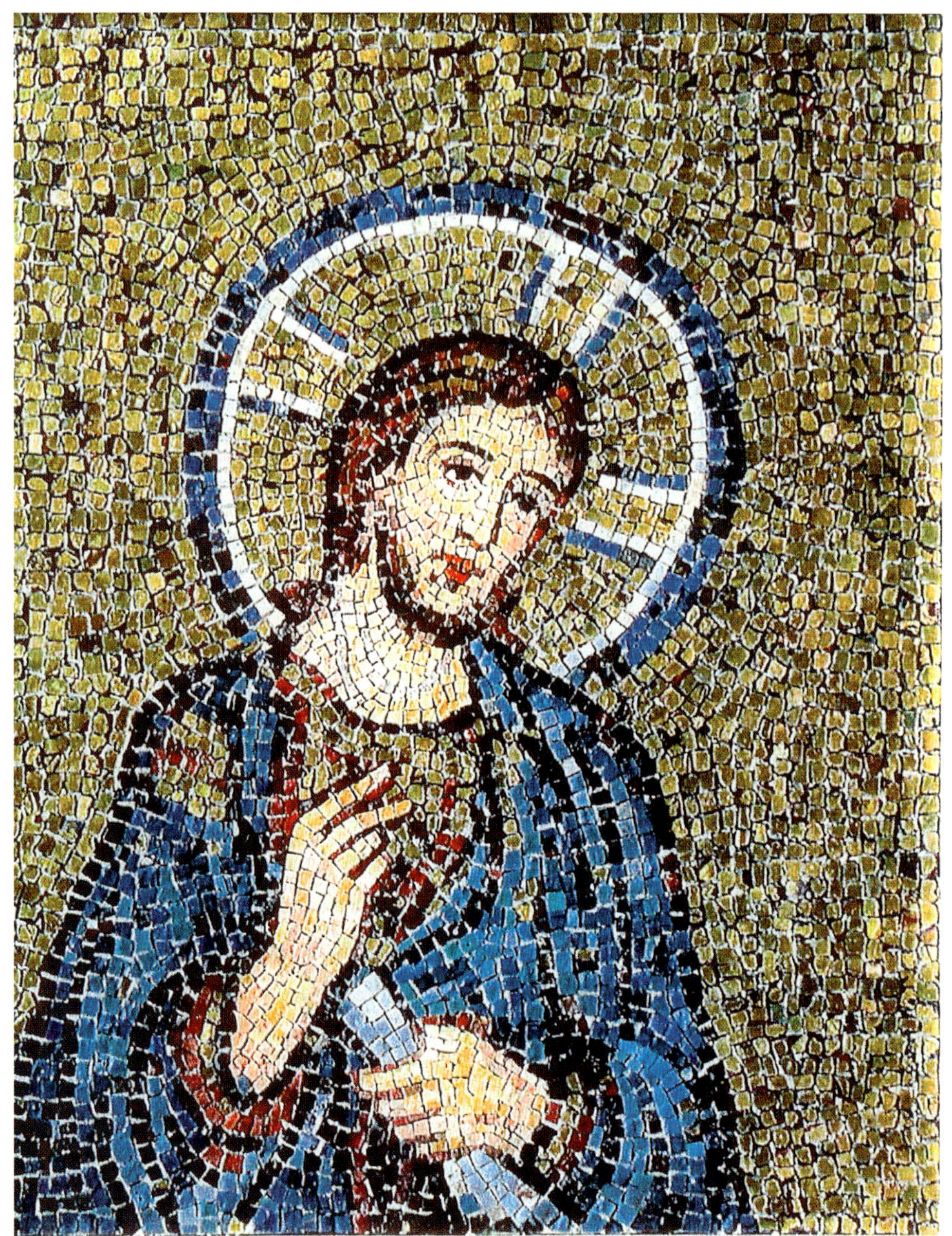

ENTRY IN JERUSALEM

cm. 65,5x75,5.
Technique in cut natural stones and enamels applied
with acrylic resin onto a marble support tray.
Reproduction from the mosaic cycle decorating the Oratory
of Pope John VII once belonging to the Constantinian Basilica, 8th century A.D.;
Vatican Grottoes collection, Vatican City.

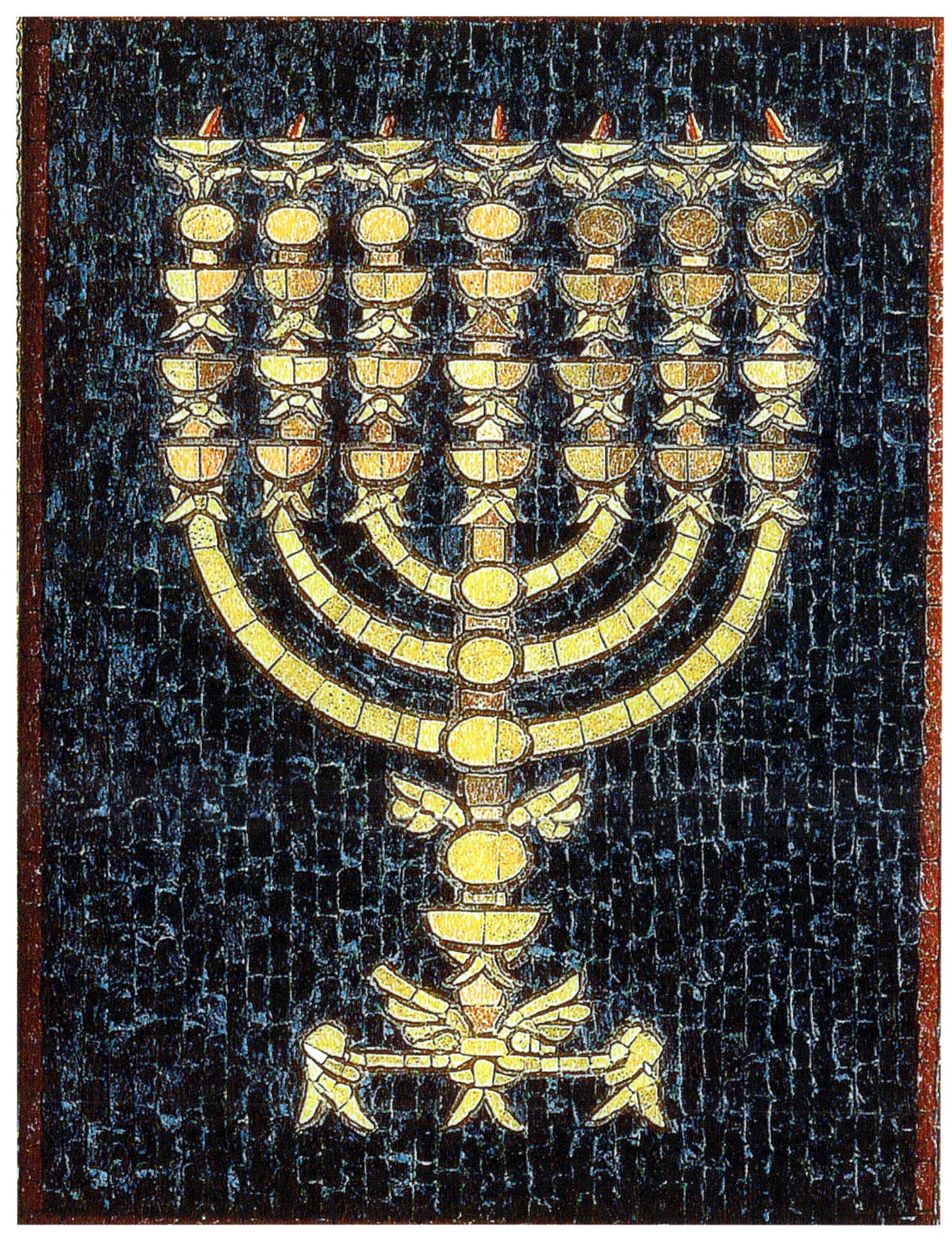

MENORAH

cm. 18x24.
Filament enamel technique applied with oily stucco onto an iron support tray.
Reproduction from an illuminated Codex, 14th century A.D. (Corbis photo archives collection).

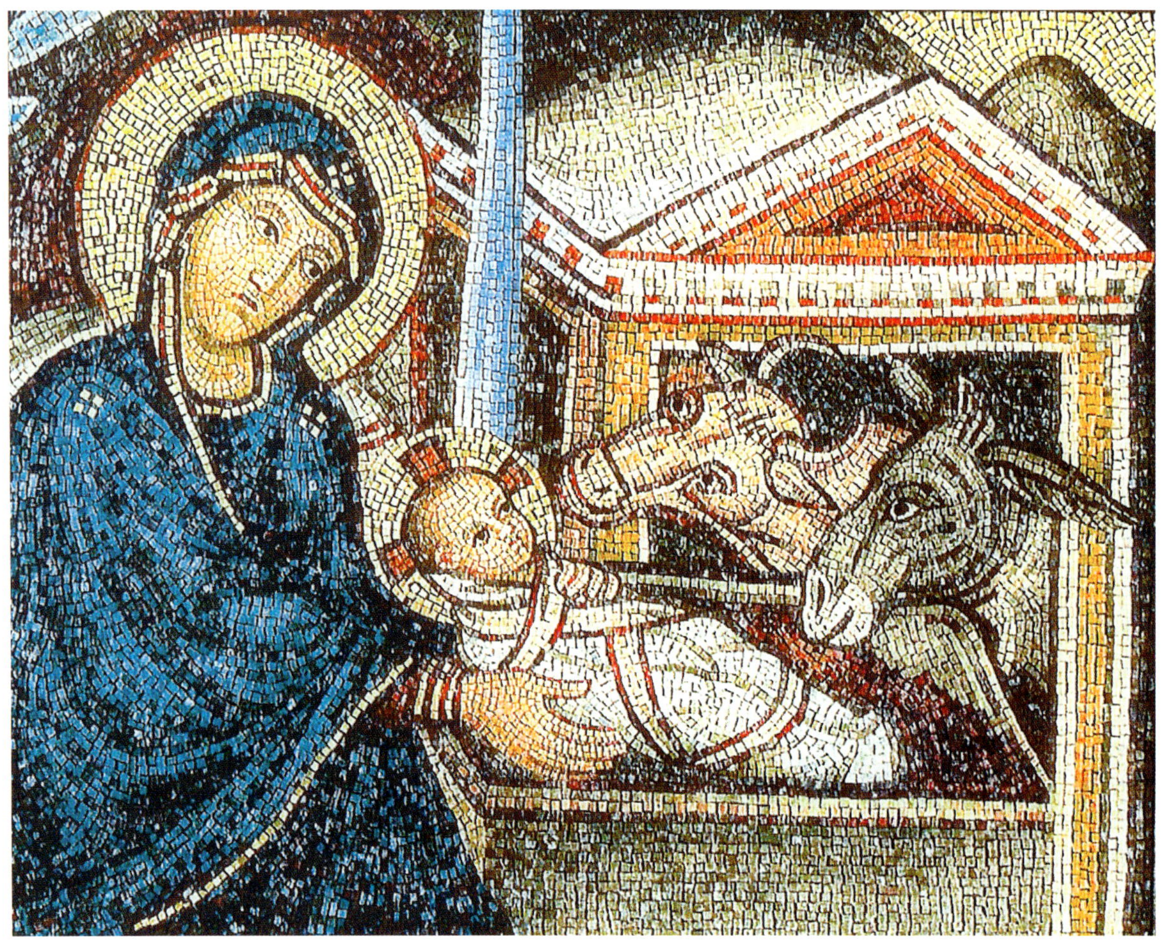

NATIVITY

cm. 74x60.
Cut enamel technique applied
with oily stucco onto an iron support tray.
Reproduction from a detail of the apse mosaic cycle,
13th century A.D.;
St. Mary Major Basilica, Rome.

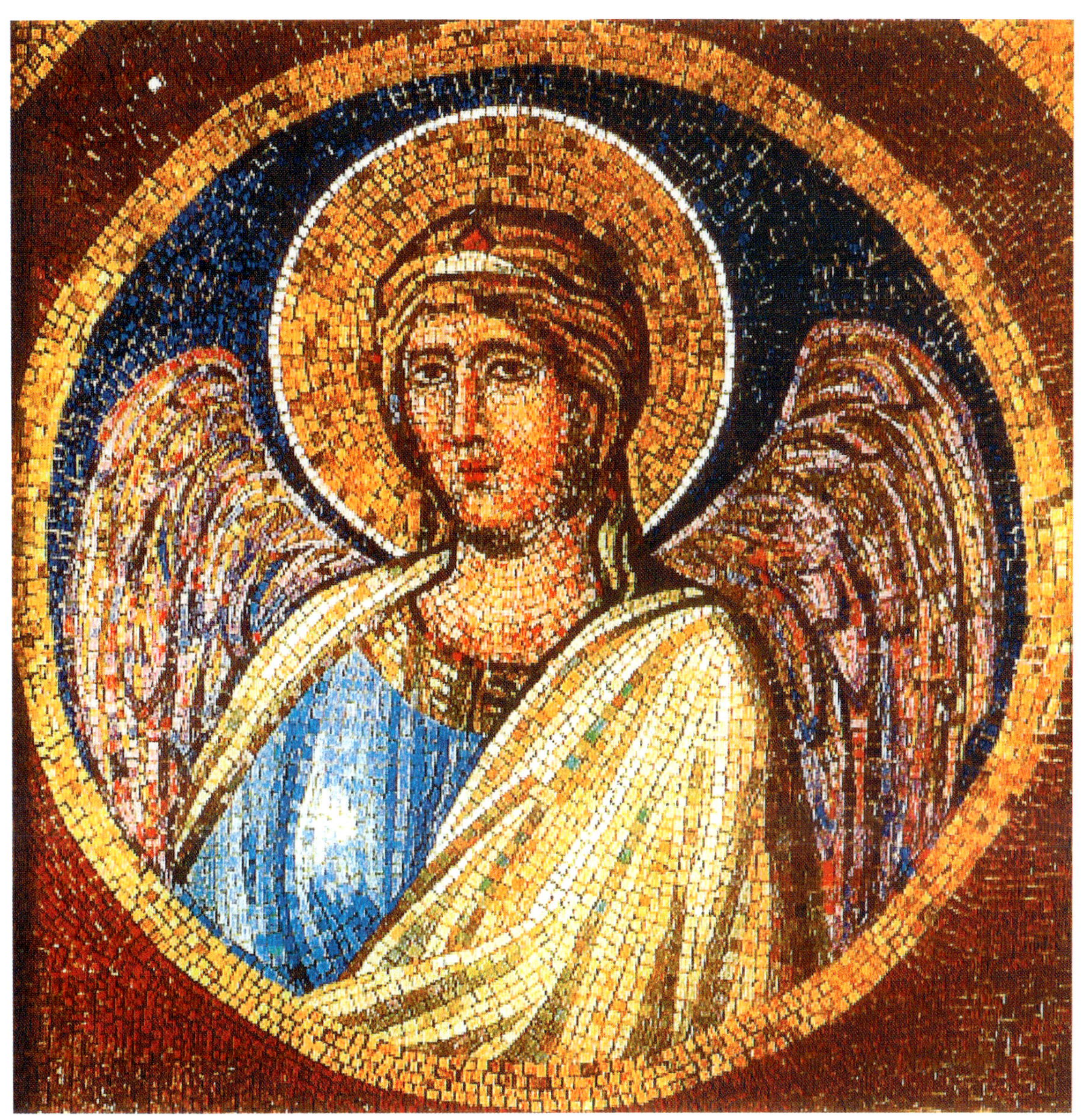

ANGEL

cm. 80x82.
Technique in cut natural stones, gilt glass, enamels,
applied with oily stucco onto a marble support tray.
Reproduction from a detail of the Navicella mosaic panel
attributed to Giotto or his workshop,
13th-14th century A.D.;
Partorienti Chapel, Vatican Grottoes collection, Vatican City.

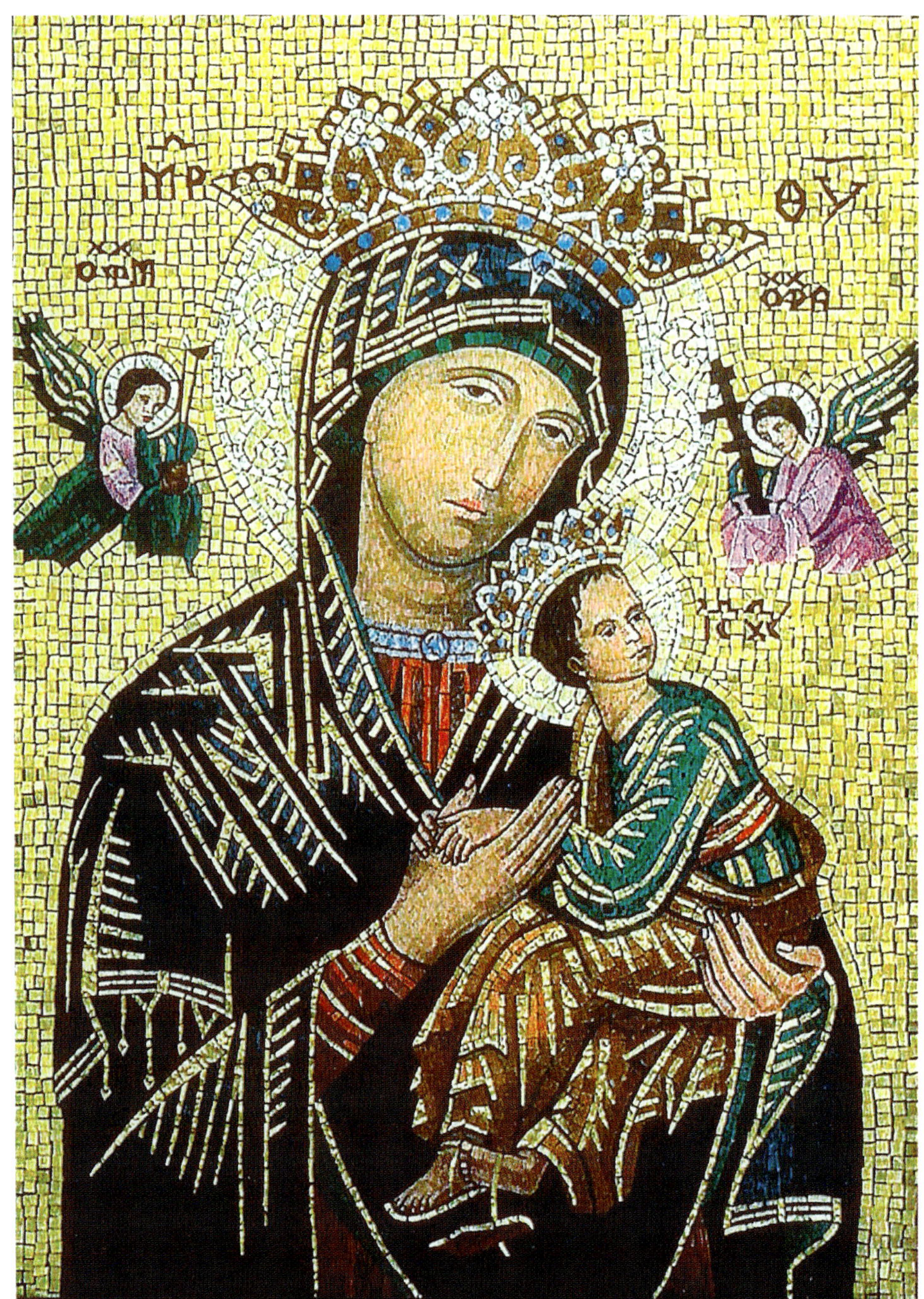

VIRGIN OF PERPETUAL HELP

cm.60x75.
Filament enamel technique, enamels and gilt glass applied with oily stucco onto an iron support tray.
Reproduction of icon, uncertain date;
St. Alfonso de' Liguori, Rome.

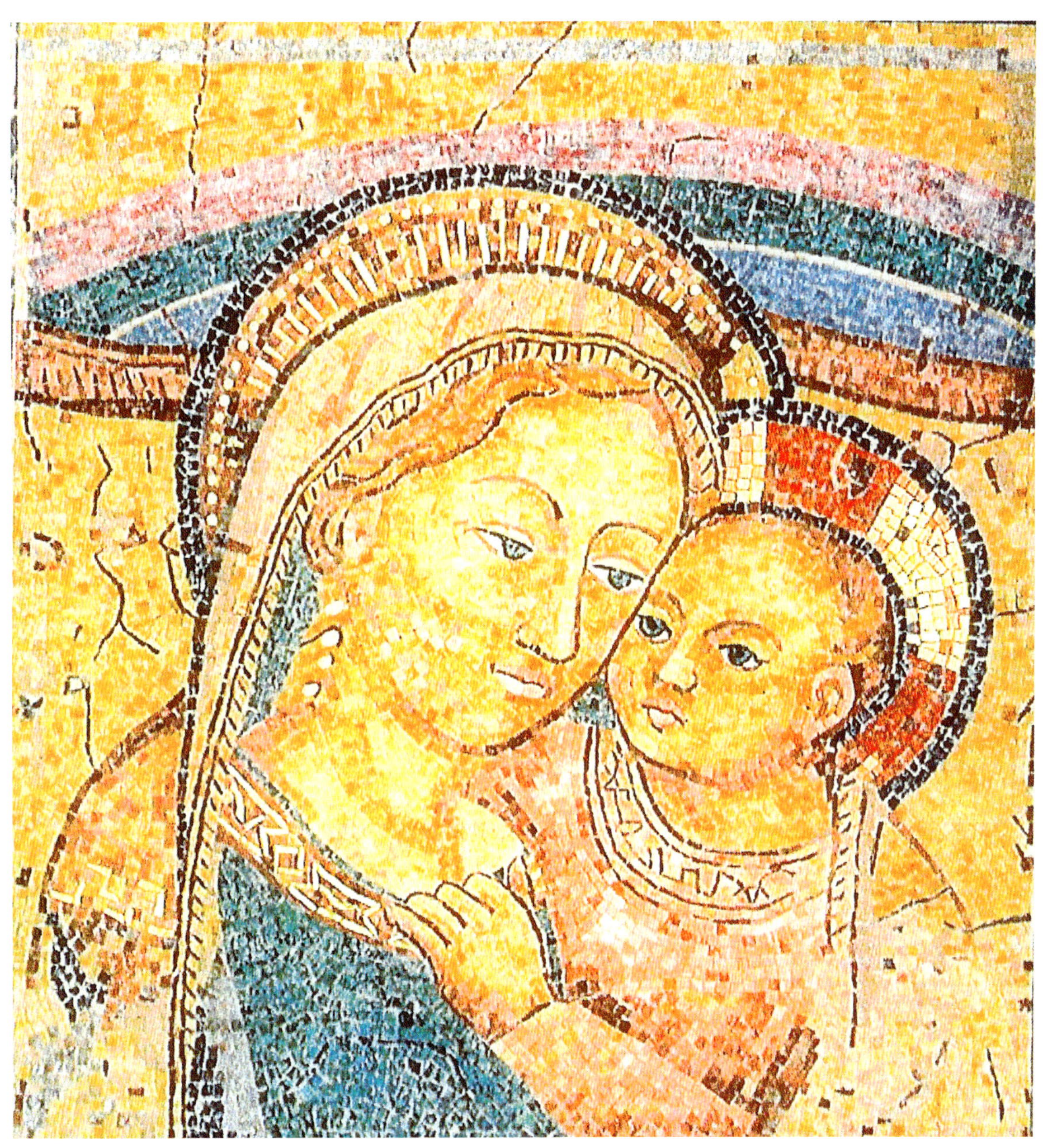

VIRGIN OF GOOD COUNSEL

cm. 60x57.
Technique in cut natural stones and gilt glass applied with acrylic resin onto a marble support tray.
Reproduction from wall fresco, 15th century A.D.;
Church of Good Counsel, Genazzano (Rome).
Courtesy of Mr. Charles Mires.

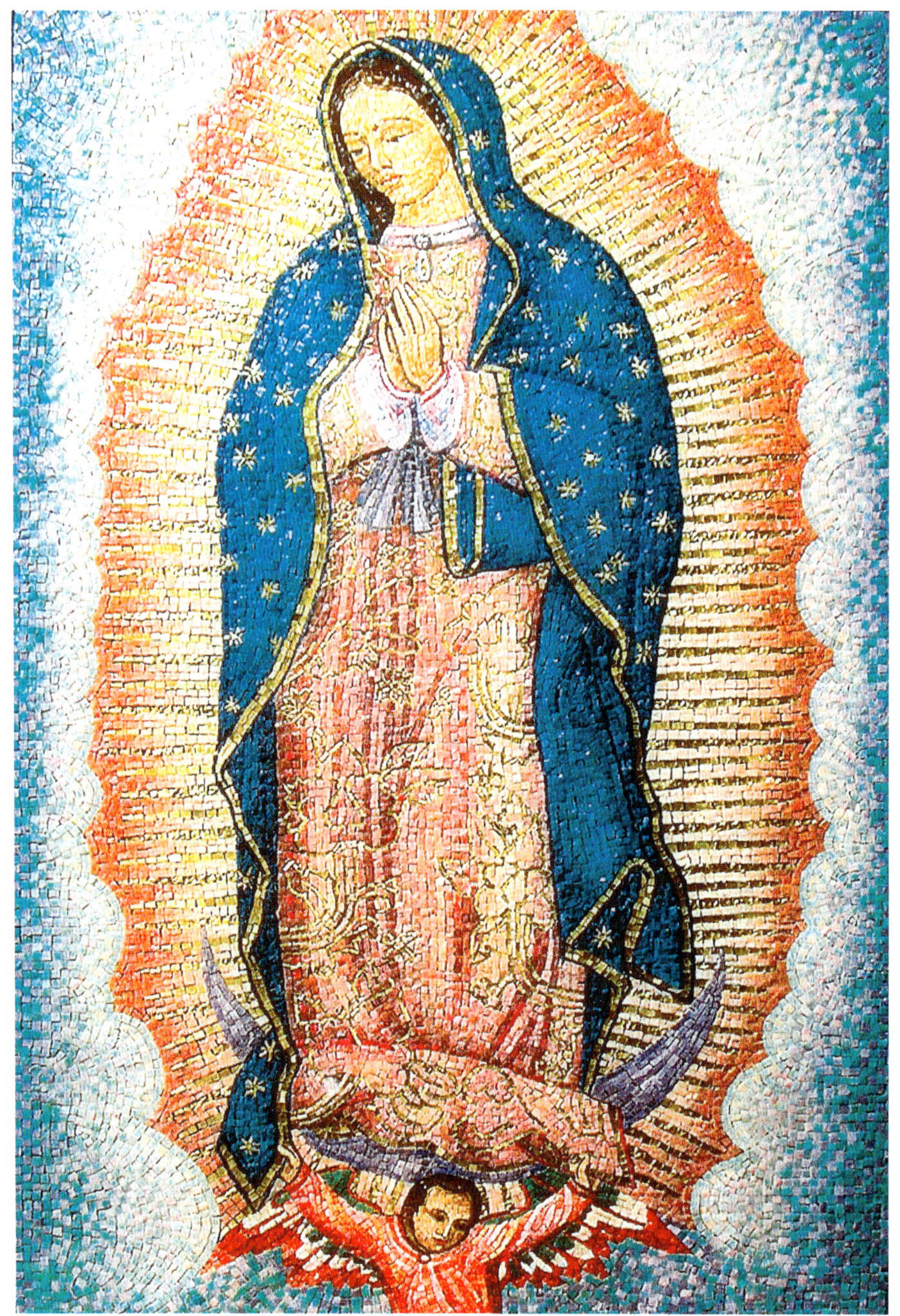

VIRGIN OF GUADALUPE

cm. 45x72.

Cut enamel technique applied with oily stucco onto an iron support tray.

Reproduction from the painted relic,

16th century A.D.; Sanctuary Madonna of Guadalupe, Mexico City.

Courtesy of Mr. Eugenio Galindo.

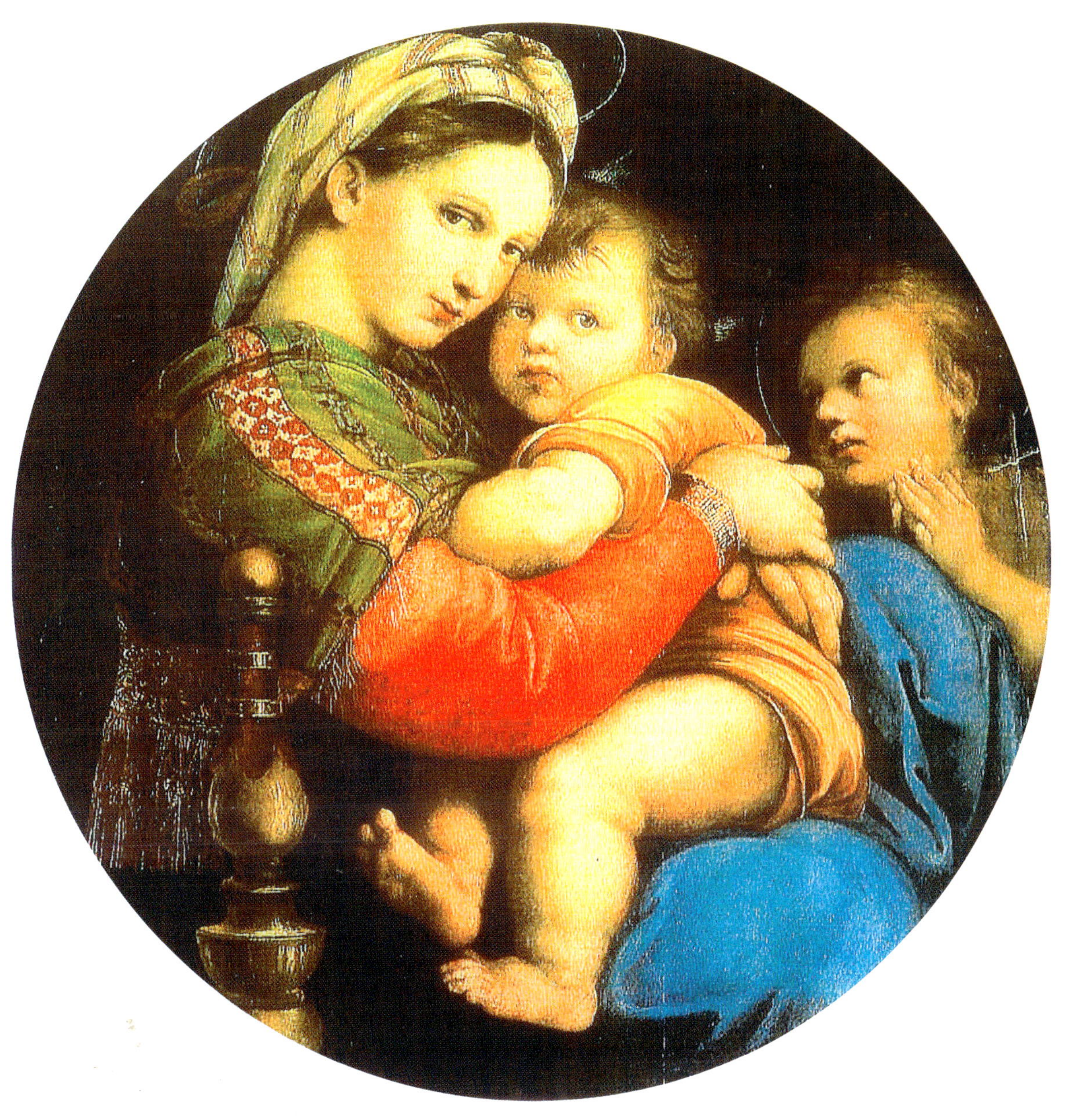

VIRGIN OF THE CHAIR

cm. 73x73.
Cut and filament enamel technique and gilt glass fixed with oily stucco onto an iron support tray.
Reproduction from the painting by Raphael, 1513-1514;
Palazzo Pitti collection, Florence.
Courtesy of William Close.

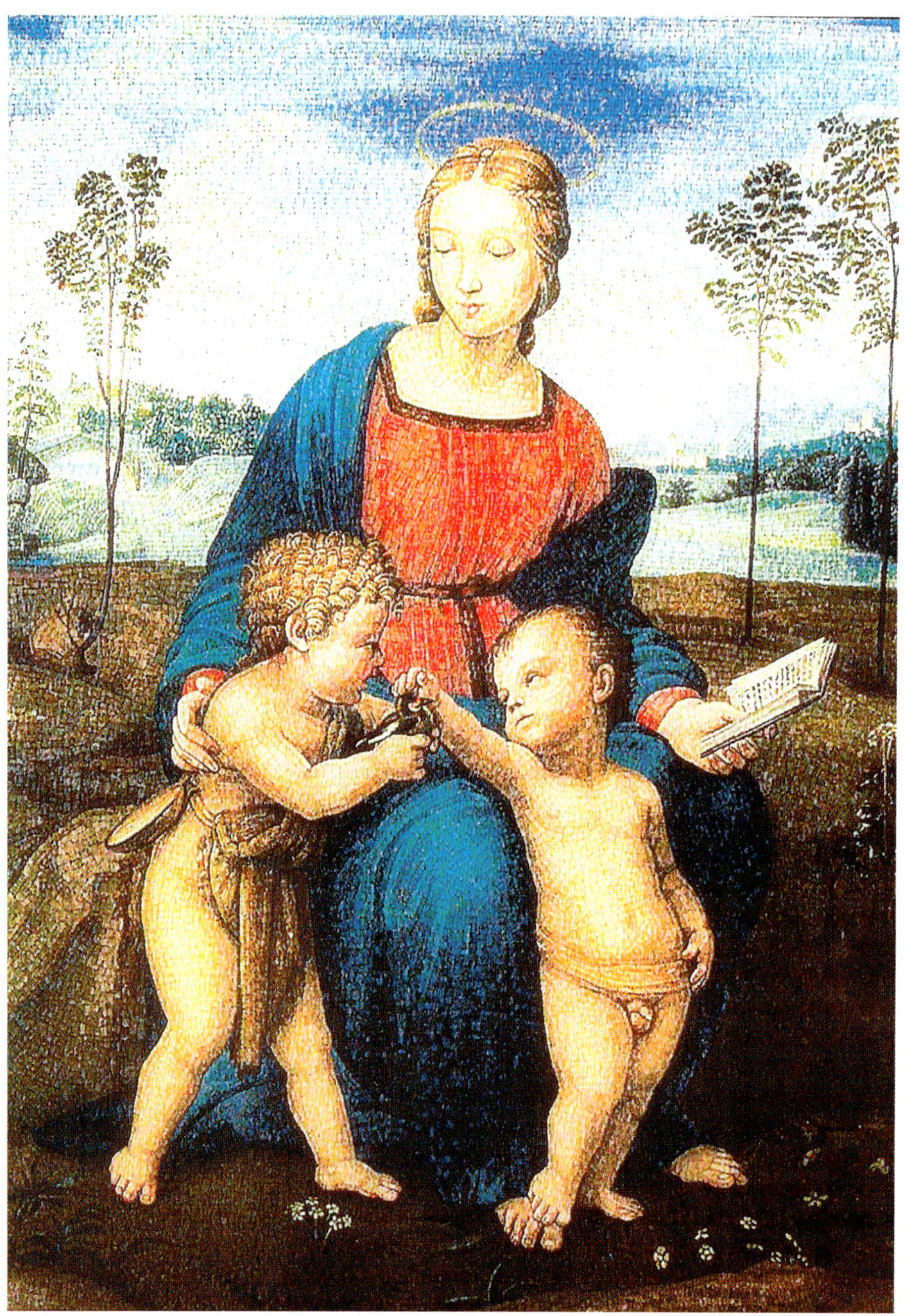

VIRGIN OF THE GOLDFINCH

cm 80x104.

Cut and filament enamel technique fixed with oily stucco onto an iron support tray.

Reproduction from the painting by Raphael, 1507;

Uffizi Gallery collection, Florence.

Courtesy of Ms. Julie Mills.

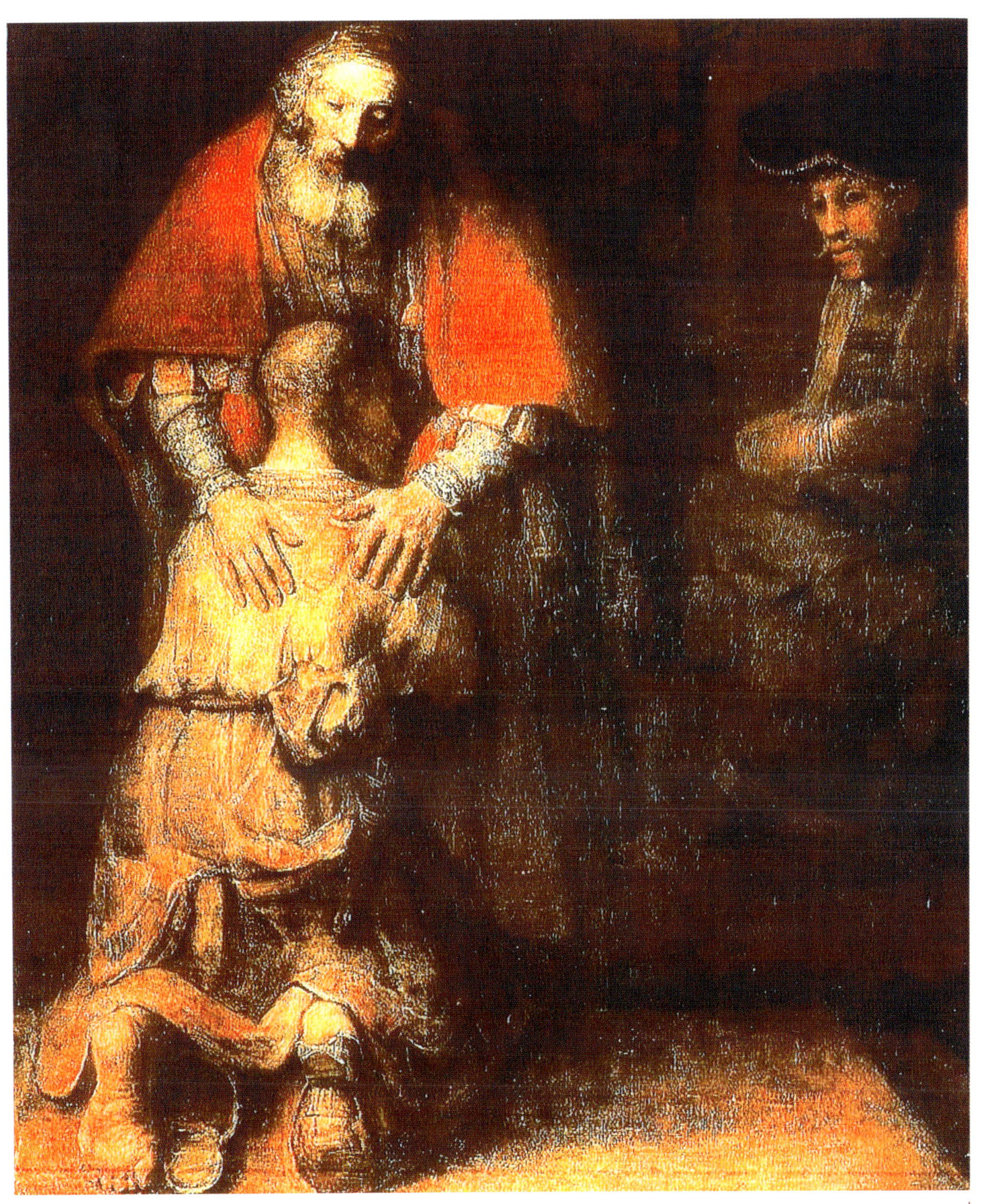

THE PRODIGAL SON

cm. 60x35.
Filament enamel technique, fixed with oily stucco onto an iron support tray.
Reproduction from detail of the painting by Rembrandt, 1669;
Hermitage Museum collection, St. Petersburg.
Courtesy of Ms. Julie Mills.

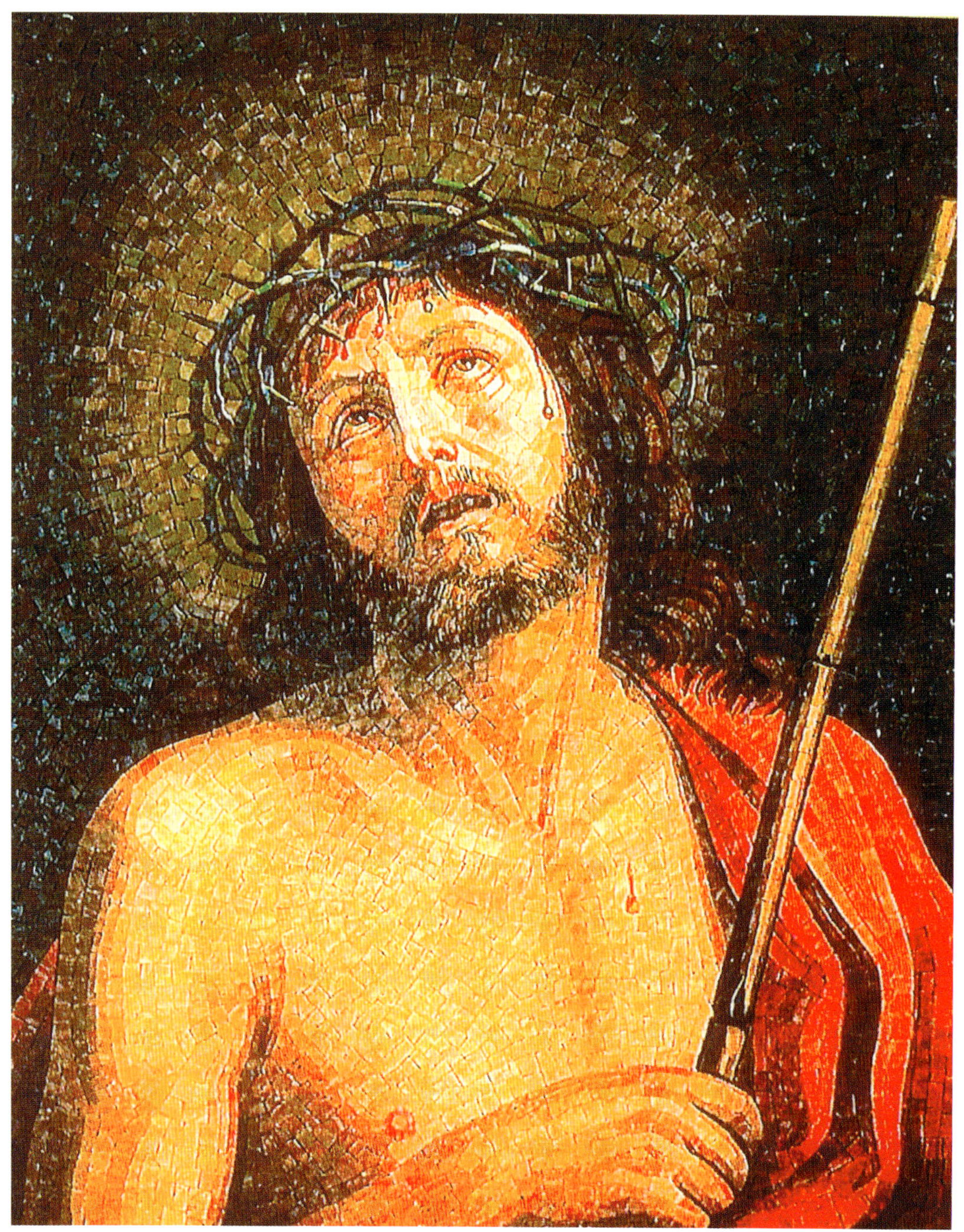

ECCE HOMO

cm. 40x50.

Cut and filament enamel technique, fixed with oily stucco onto an iron support tray.

Reproduction of a painting attributed to Guercino or his workshop,

17th century A.D.;

from a study in the archives collection of the Vatican Mosaic Studio.

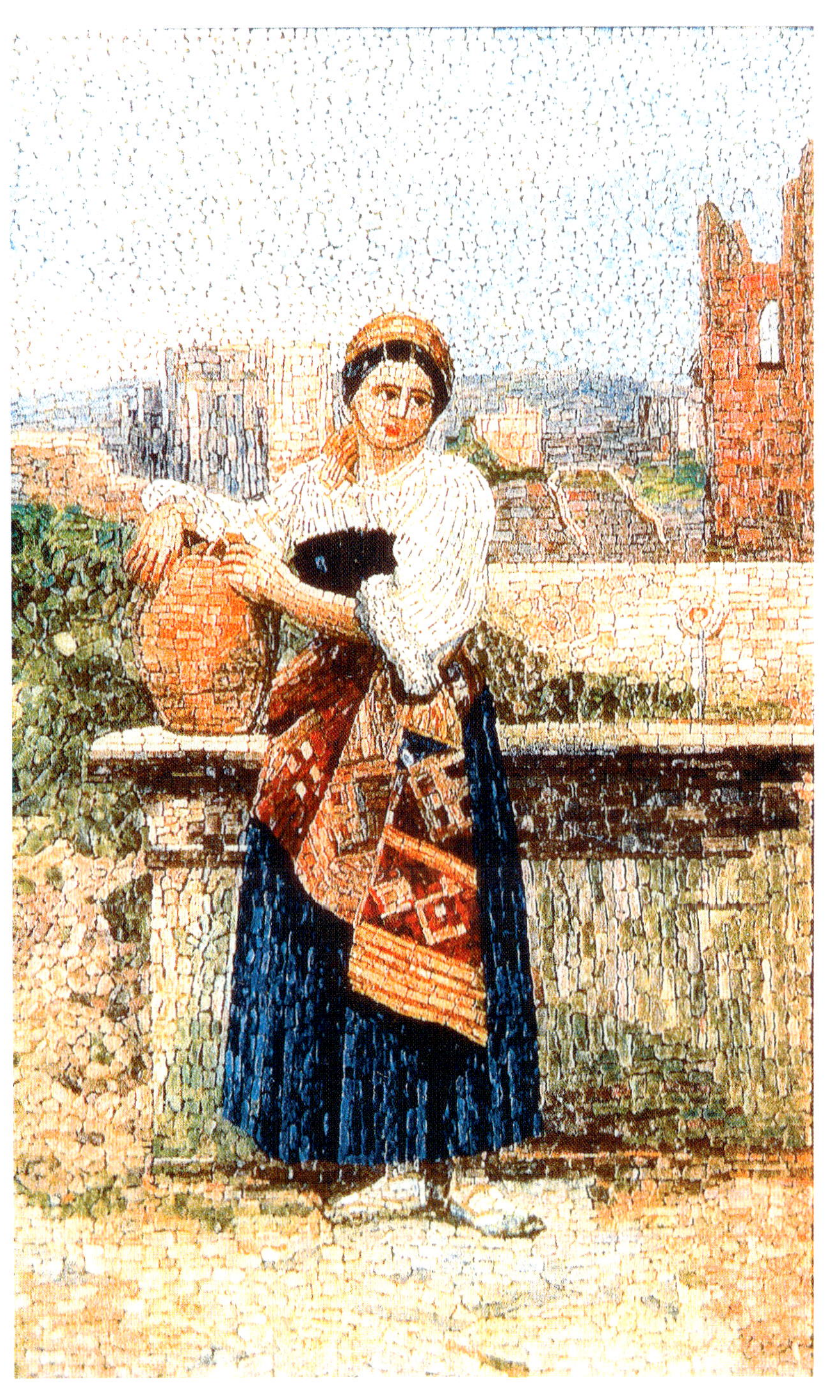

WOMAN AT WELL

cm. 18x28.

Filament enamel technique, fixed with oily stucco onto an iron support tray. Reproduction from the painting by Augusto Bompiani, 19th-20th century A.D.; photo archives collection of the Vatican Mosaic Studio, Vatican City.

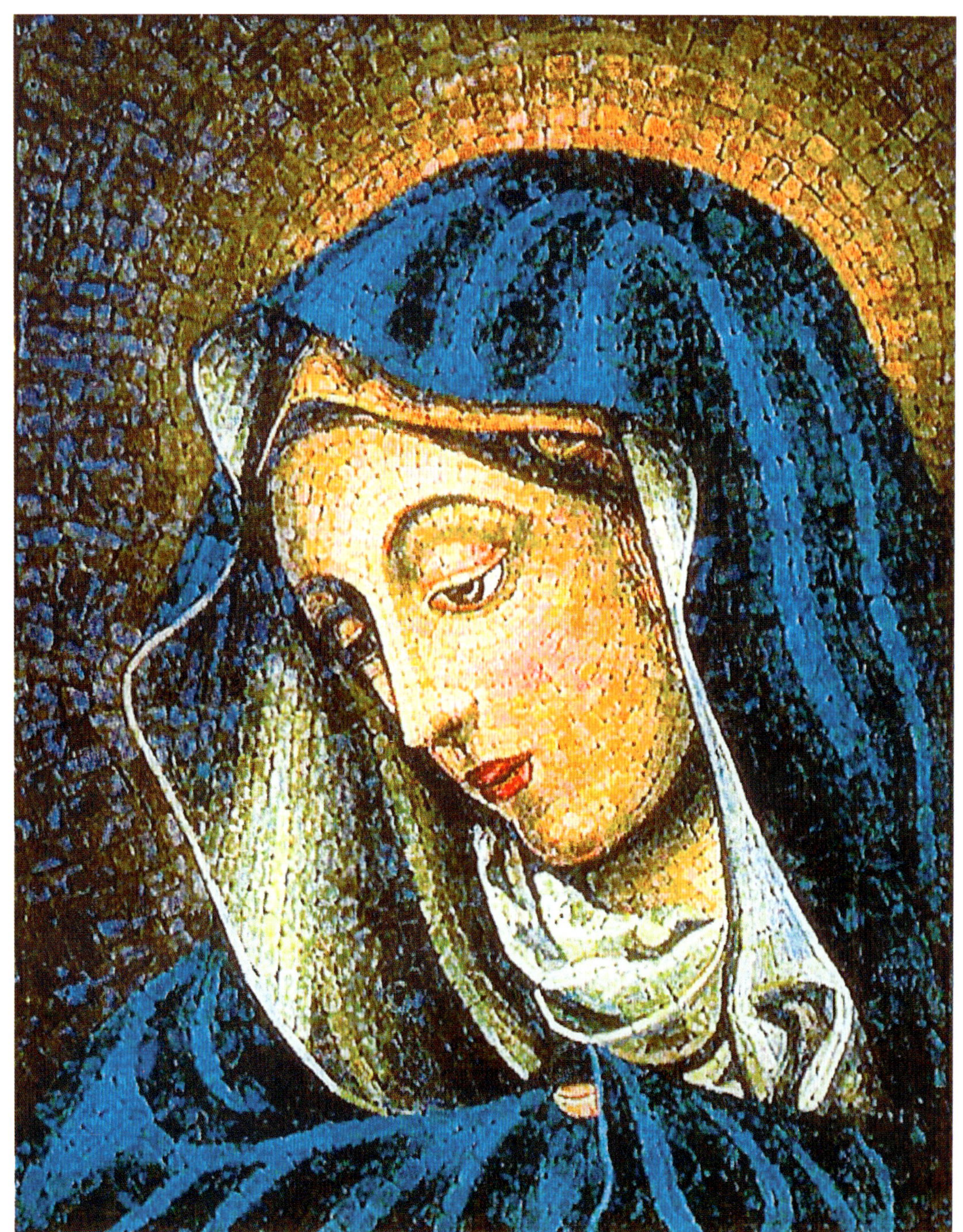

VIRGIN OF THE FINGER

cm. 16x12.

Filament enamel technique, fixed with oily stucco onto an iron support tray.

Reproduction from the painting by Carlo Dolci, 17th century A.D.;

Borghese Gallery collection, Rome.

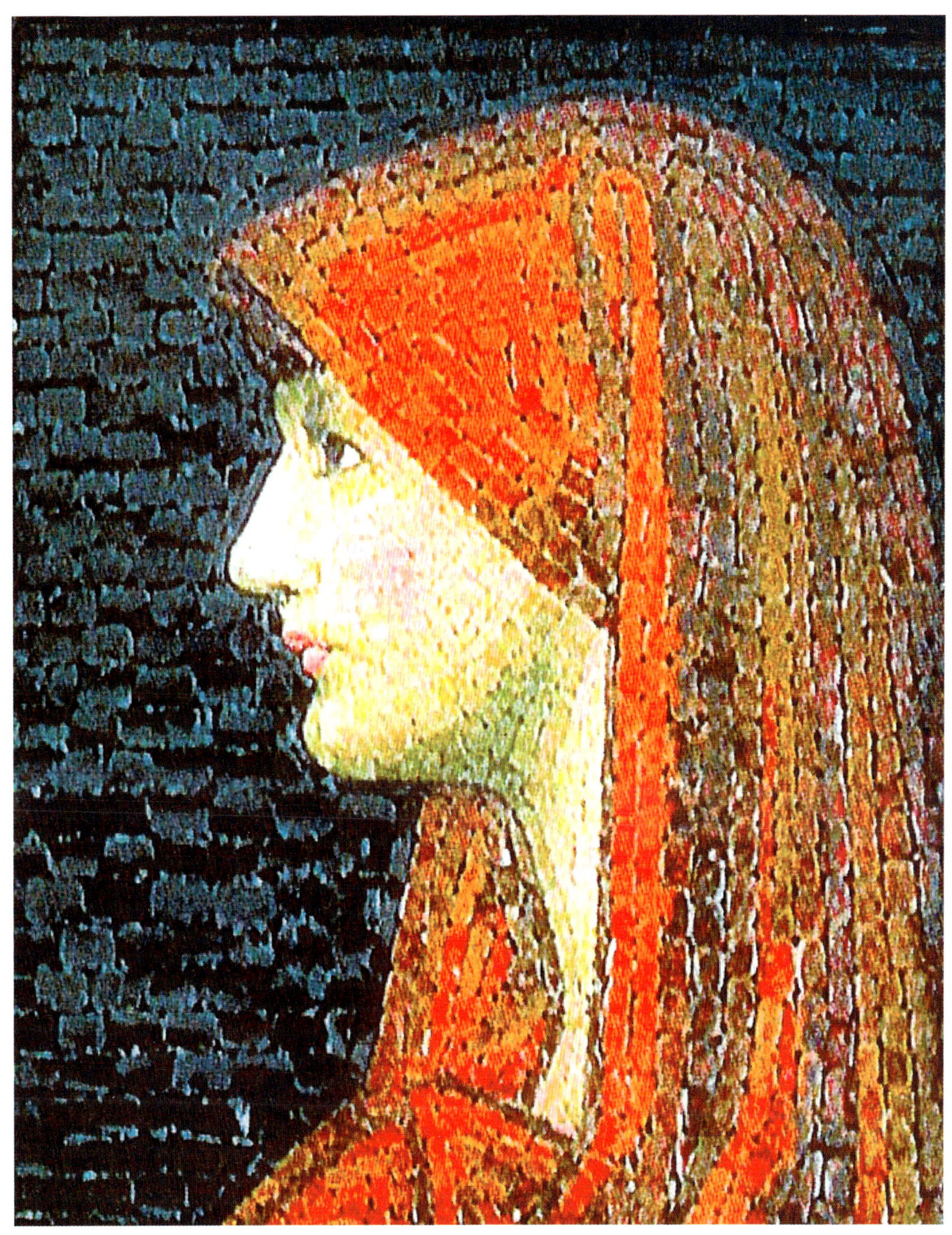

FABIOLA

cm. 13x16.

Filament enamel technique, fixed with oily stucco onto an iron support tray.

Reproduction from the painting by Jean Jacques Henner, 19th century A.D.;

Louvre Museum collection, Paris.

Courtesy of Dr. and Mrs. Harley Stock.

ST. PETER'S SQUARE

cm. 60x35.
Filament enamel technique,
fixed with oily stucco
onto an iron support tray.
Reproduction from a painting
of anonymous author,
19th century A.D.;
photo archives collection
of the Vatican Mosaic Studio.

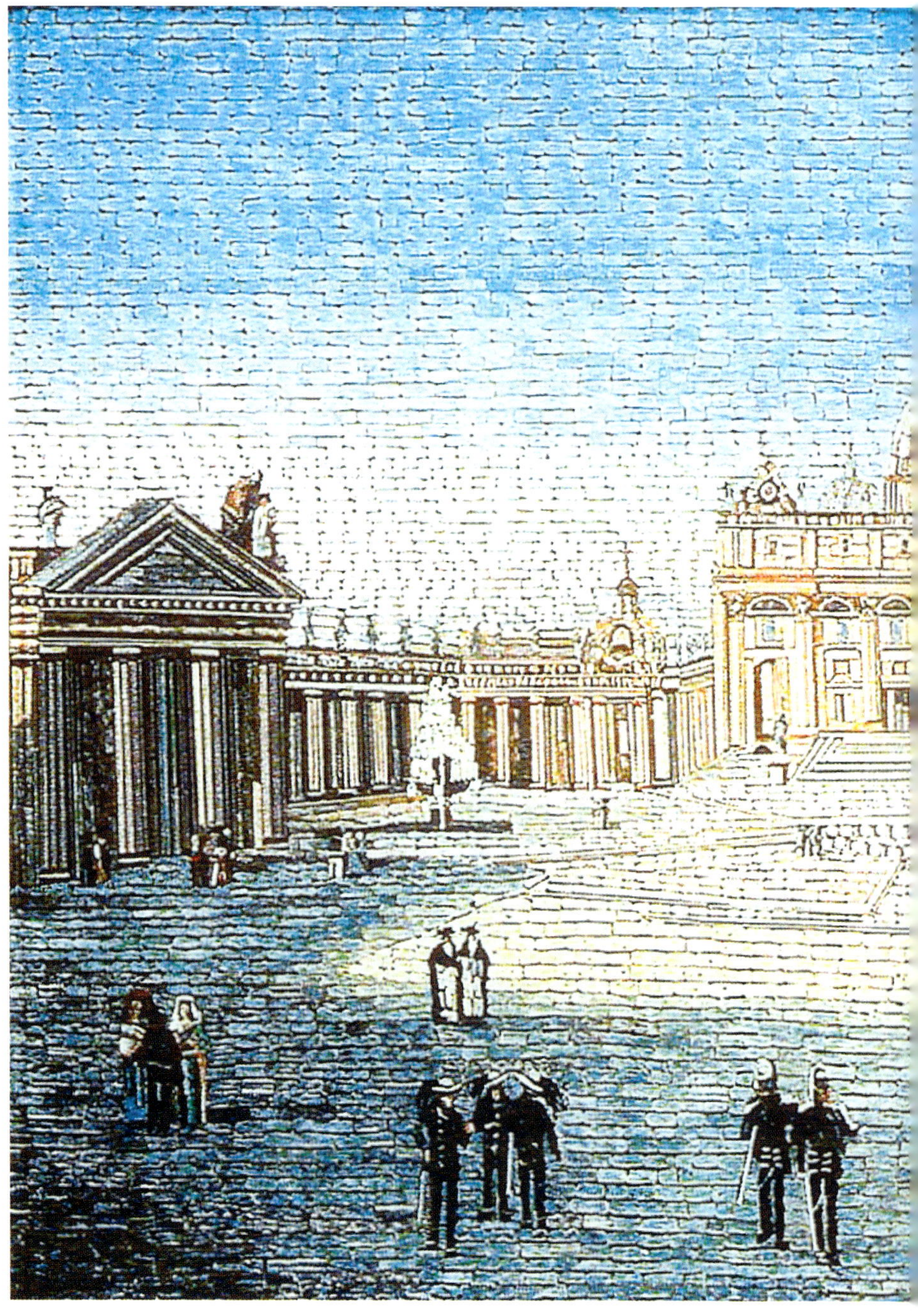

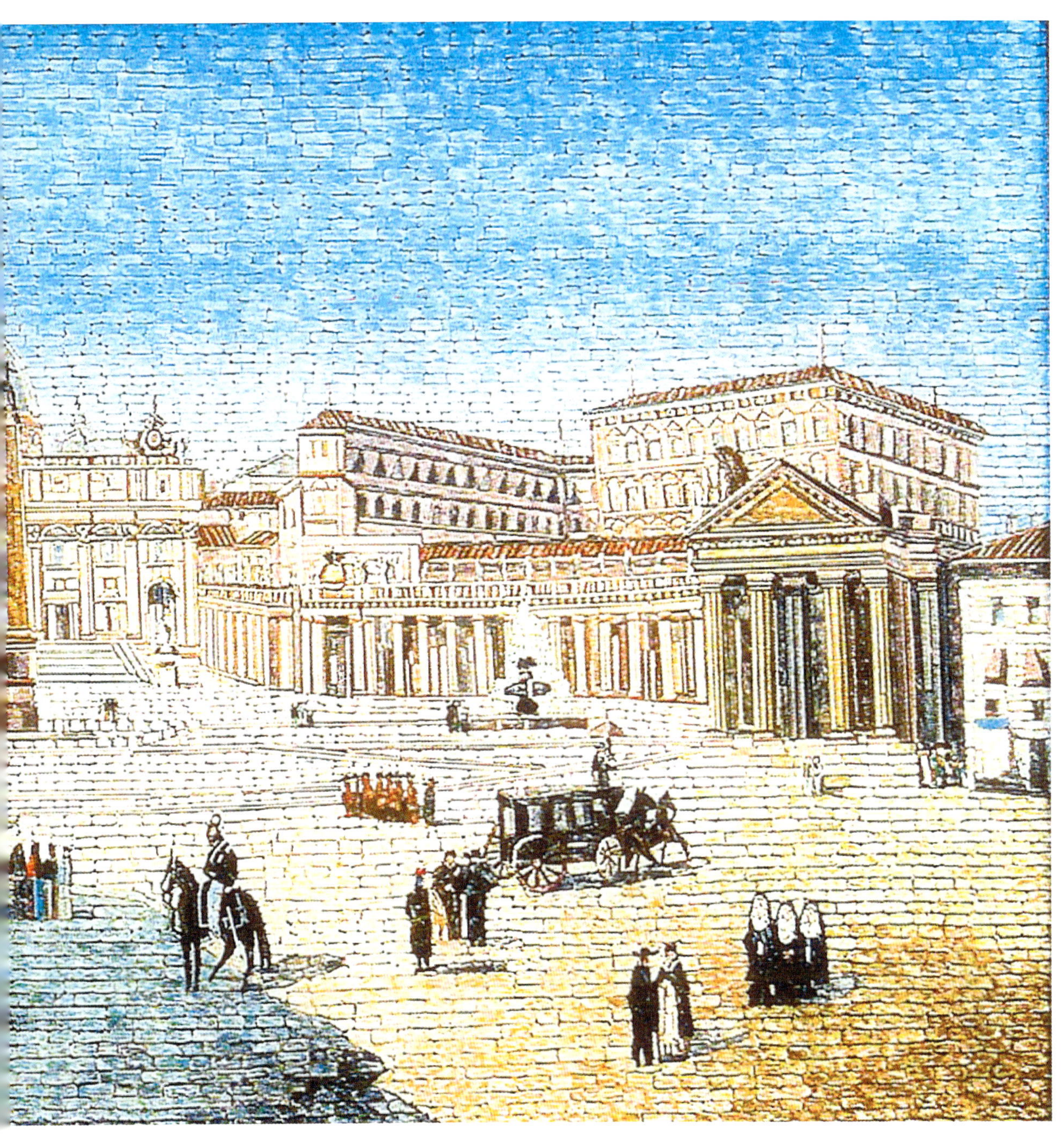

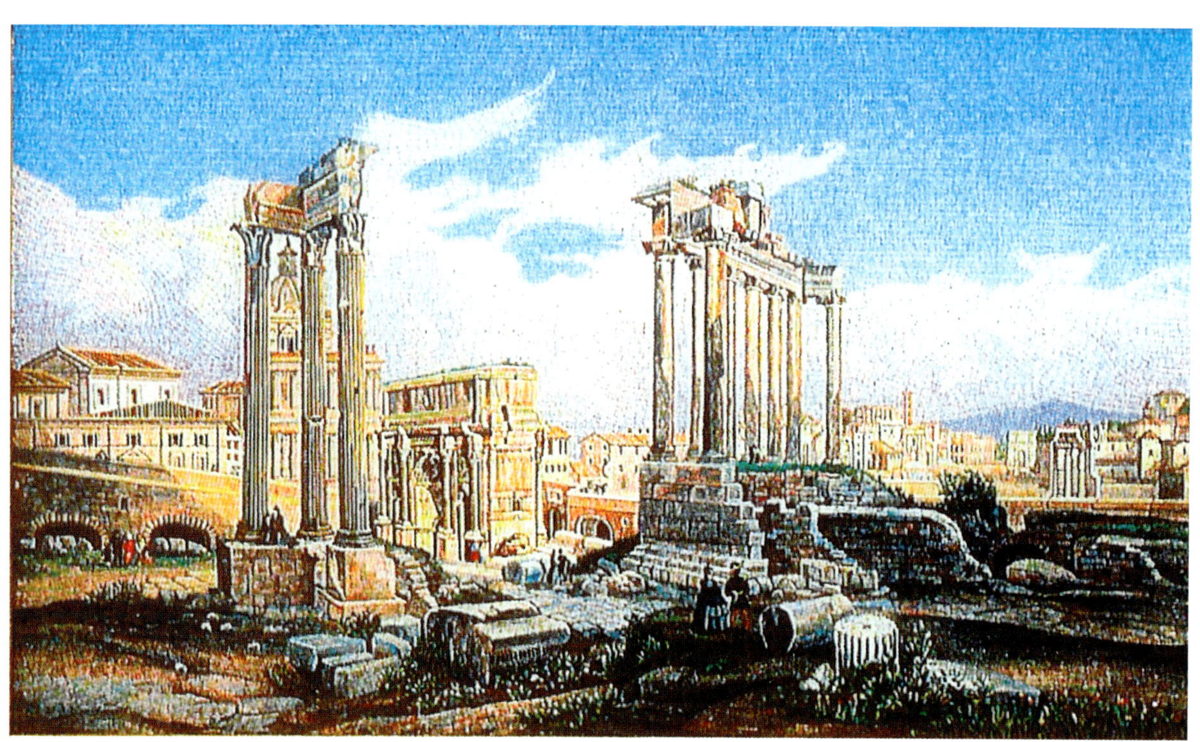

ROMAN FORUM

cm. 60x35.
Filament enamel technique,
fixed with oily stucco onto an iron support tray.
Reproduction from a painting by Ippolito Caffi,
19th century A.D.
Courtesy of Mr. and Mrs. David Collis.

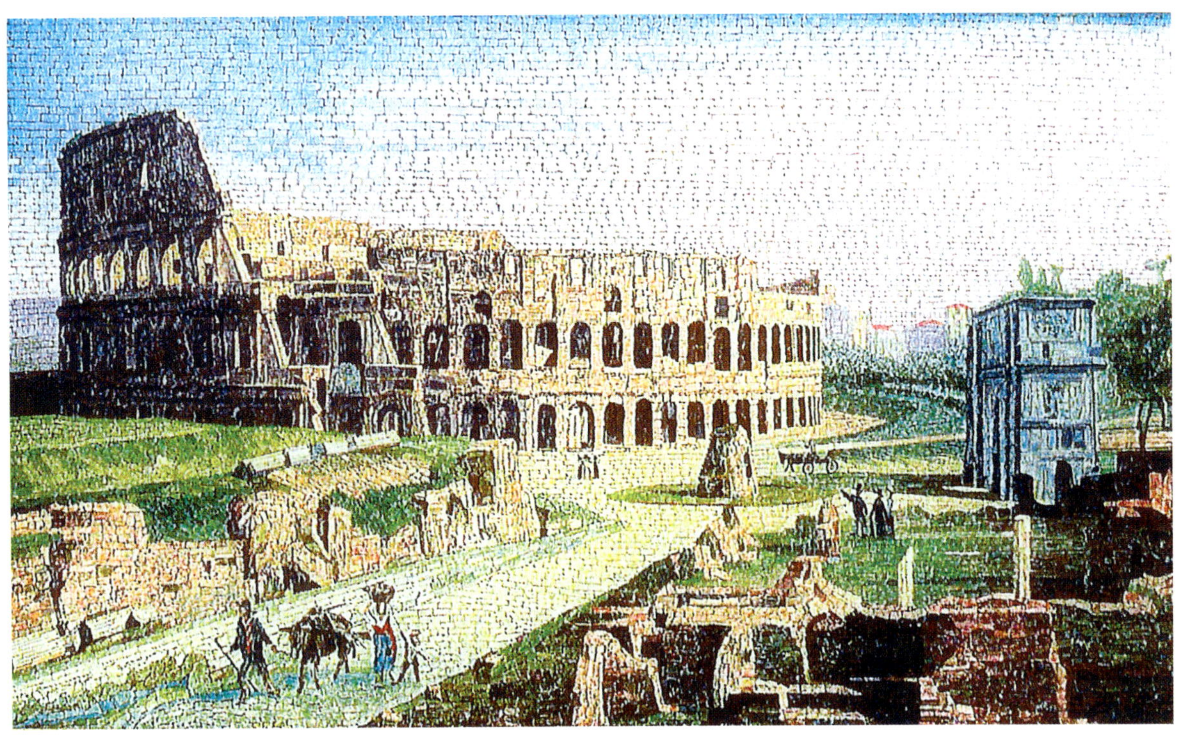

COLOSSEUM

cm. 60x35.
Filament enamel technique,
fixed with oily stucco onto an iron support tray.
Reproduction from a painting of anonymous author,
19th century A.D.;
photo archives collection of the Vatican Mosaic Studio.
Courtesy of Mr. and Mrs. David Collis.

CASTEL SANT'ANGELO AND ST. PETER BASILICA

cm. 60x35.
Filament enamel technique, fixed with oily stucco onto an iron support tray.
Reproduction from the watercolor by Ettore Roesler Franz, 19th-20th century A.D.;
Folklore Museum collection, Rome.
Courtesy of Ms. Peggy Schulze.

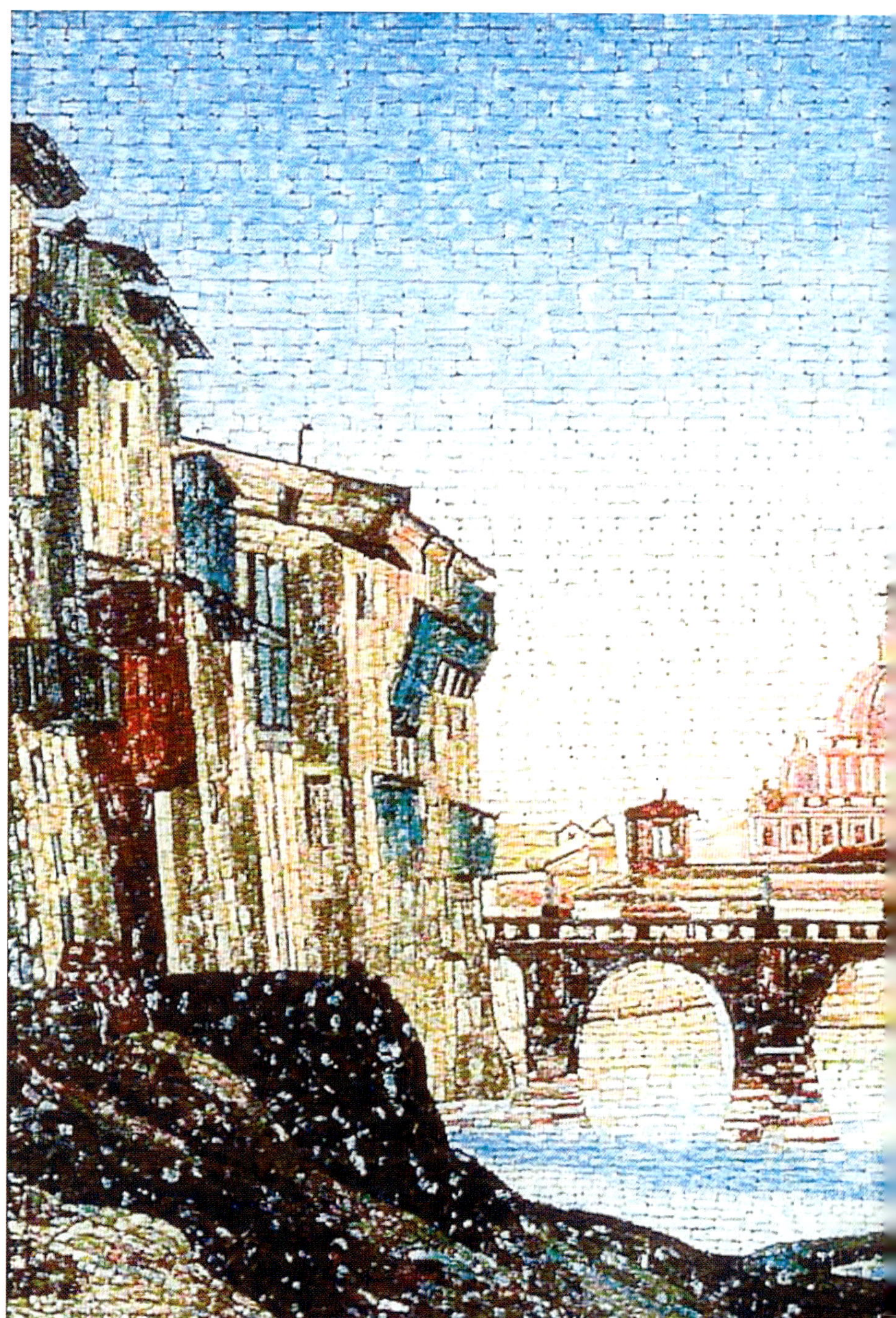

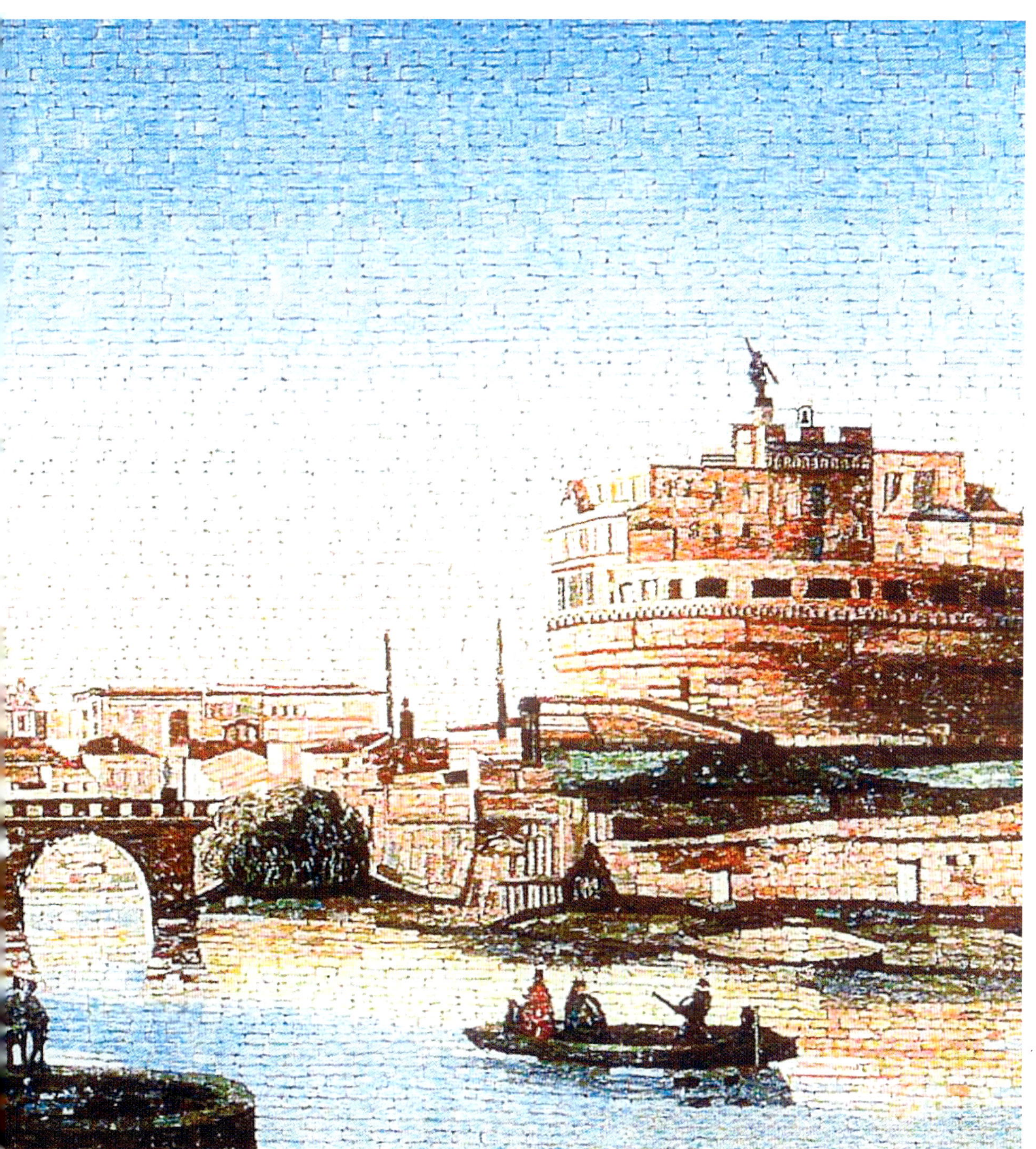

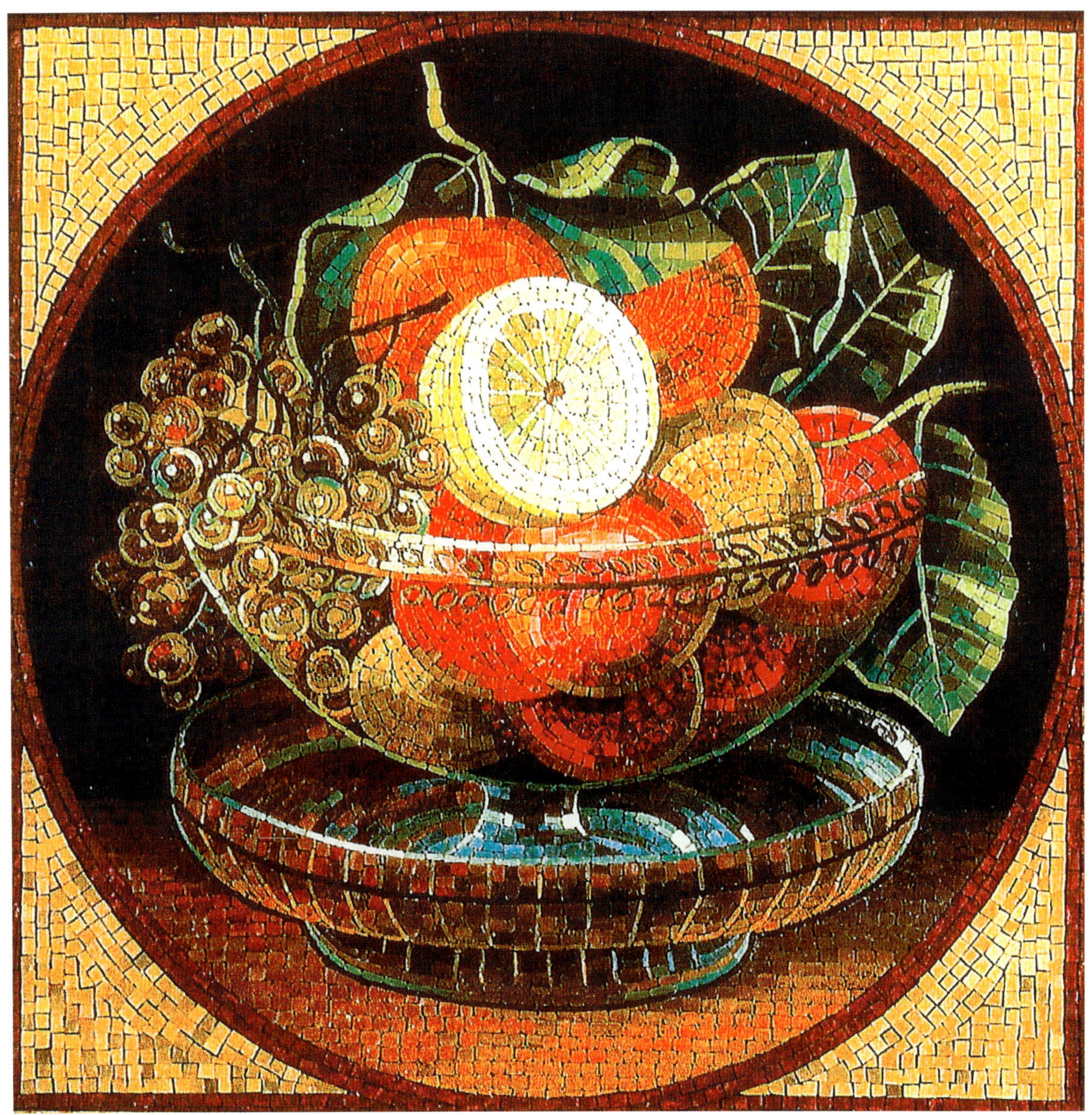

A FRUIT CUP

cm. 39x39.

Filament enamel technique, fixed with oily stucco onto an iron support tray.

Reproduction from the painting by Mantovani,

19th century A.D.; Fabbrica of St. Peter collection, Vatican City.

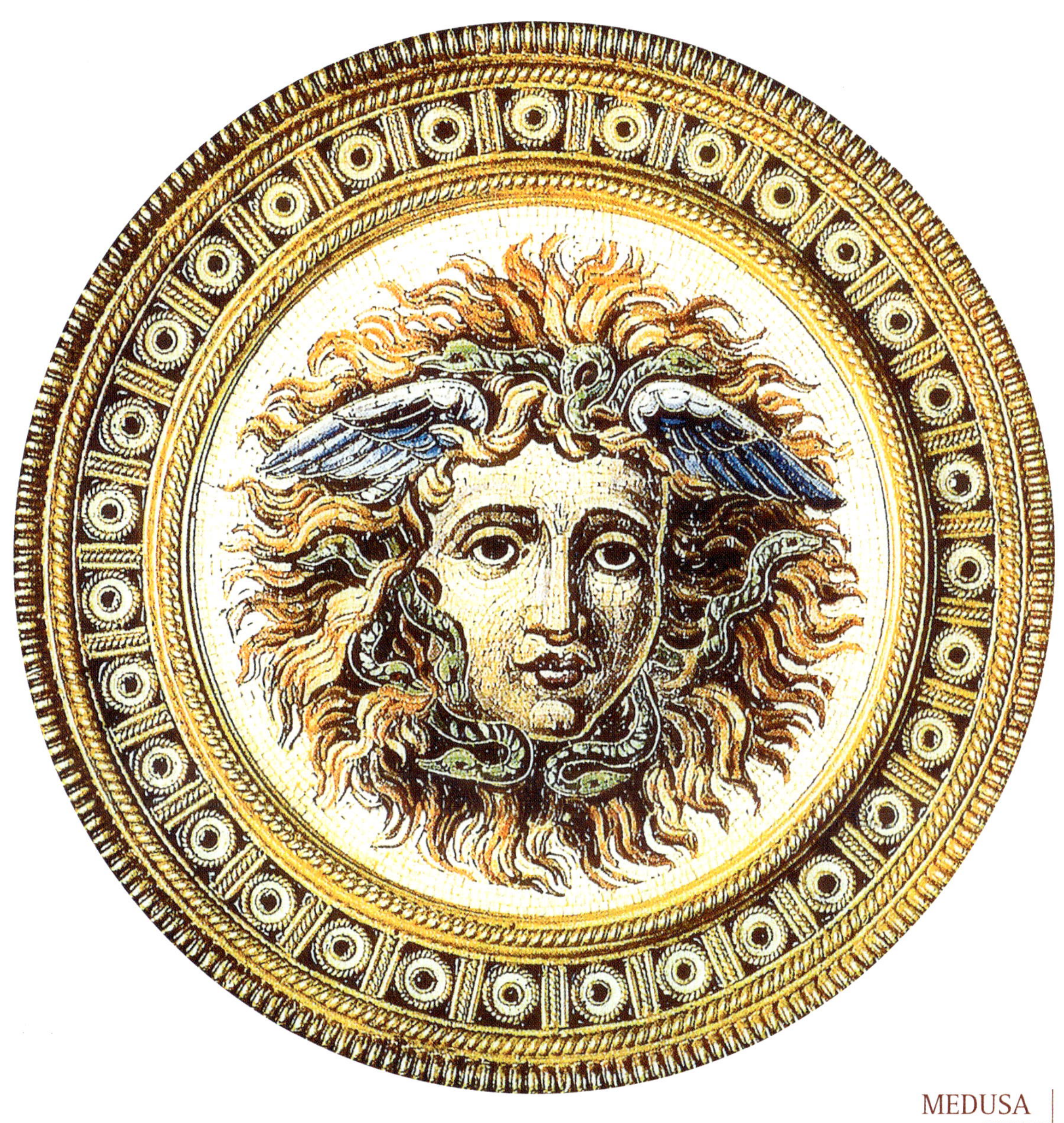

MEDUSA

diameter cm. 3,2.
Filament enamel micromosaic technique fixed
with oily stucco onto a gold support tray.
Reproduction from a micromosaic, 19th century A.D.;
in the Castellani collection, Villa Giulia Museum of Etruscan Art, Rome.

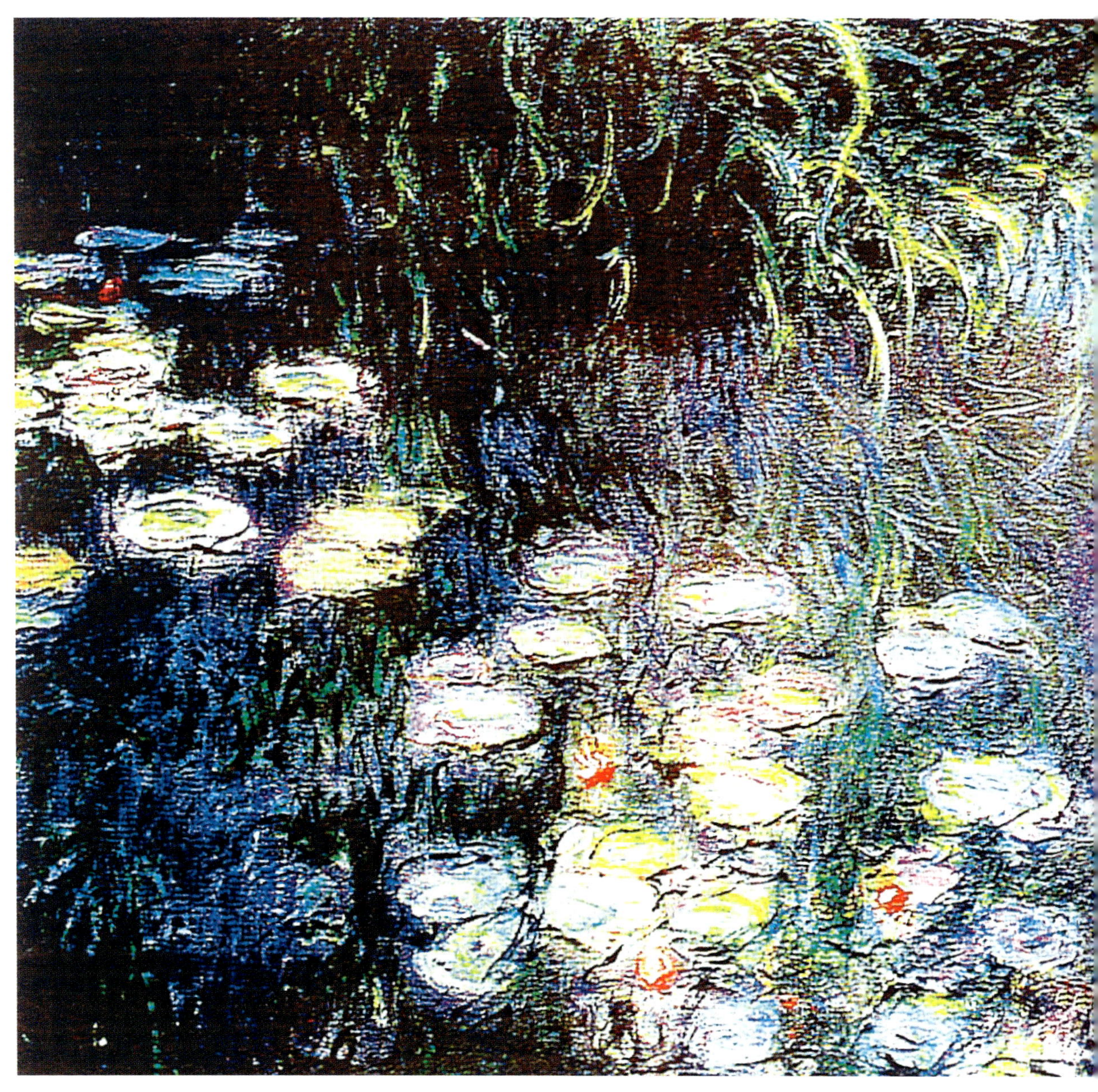

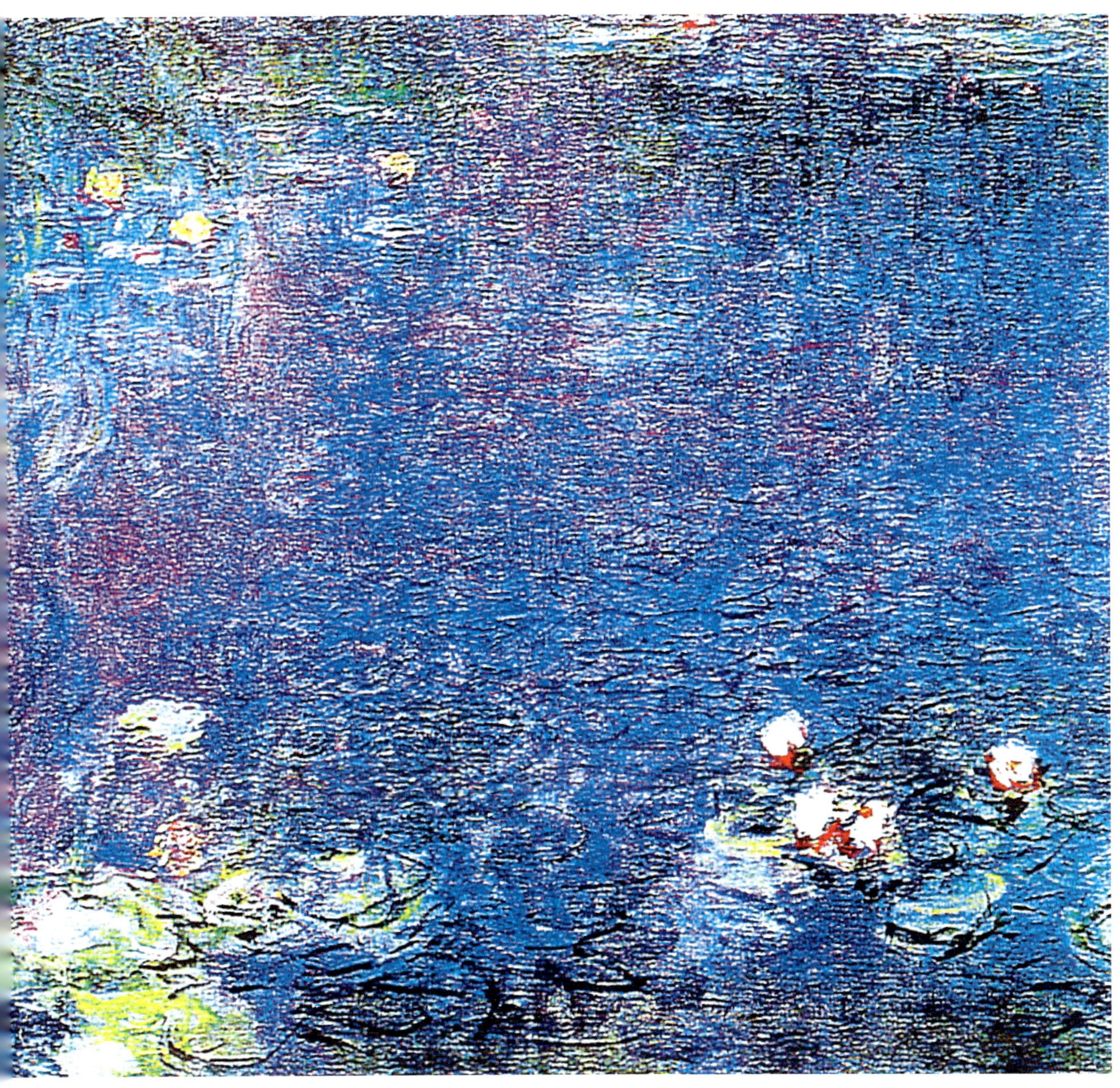

WATER LILIES

cm. 125x55.

Cut and filament enamel technique, fixed with oily stucco onto an iron support tray.

Reproduction of the painting by Claude Monet,

mid-19th century;

Orangerie Museum collection, Paris.

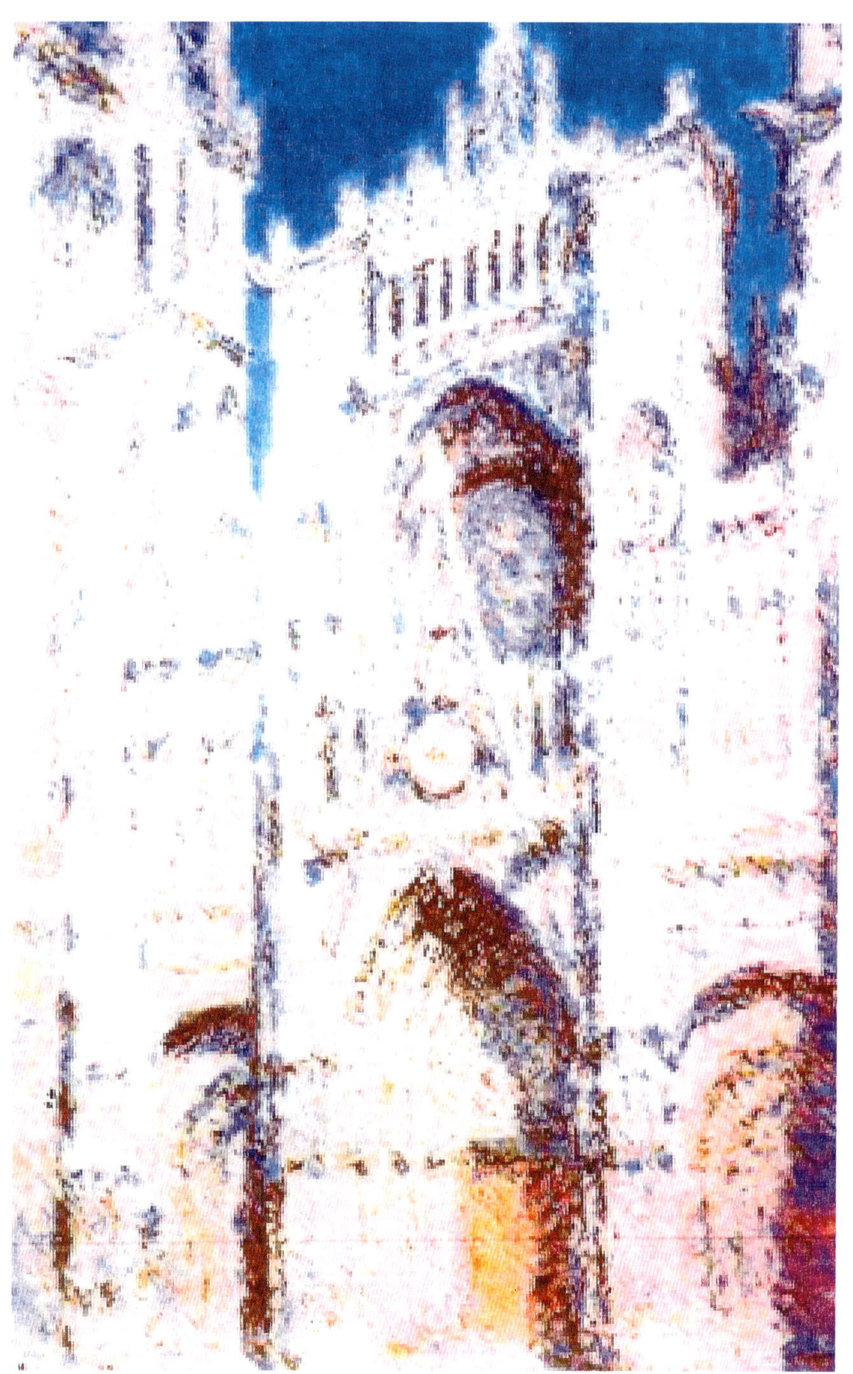

ROUEN CATHEDRAL: THE PORTAL (IN SUN)

cm. 36x55.

Cut and filament enamel technique, fixed with oily stucco onto an iron support tray.

Reproduction of the painting by Claude Monet, 1894;

Metropolitan Museum of Art collection, New York.

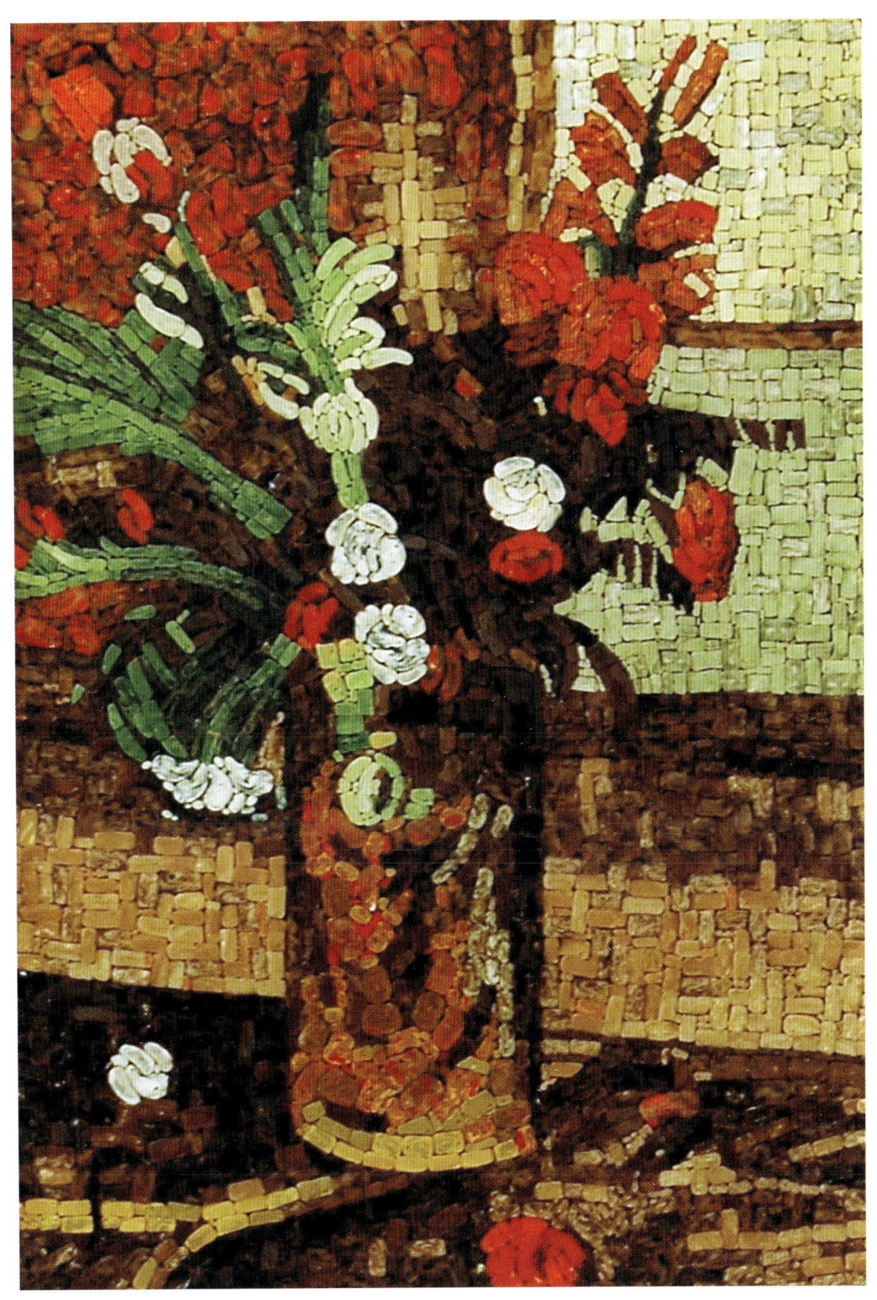

"PORTRAIT OF ESTELLE MUSSON DEGAS"

cm. 20x29.
Cut and filament enamel
technique, fixed with oily stucco onto an iron support tray.
Reproduction of a detail from the painting by Edgar Degas, 1872;
New Orleans Museum of Art collection, New Orleans.

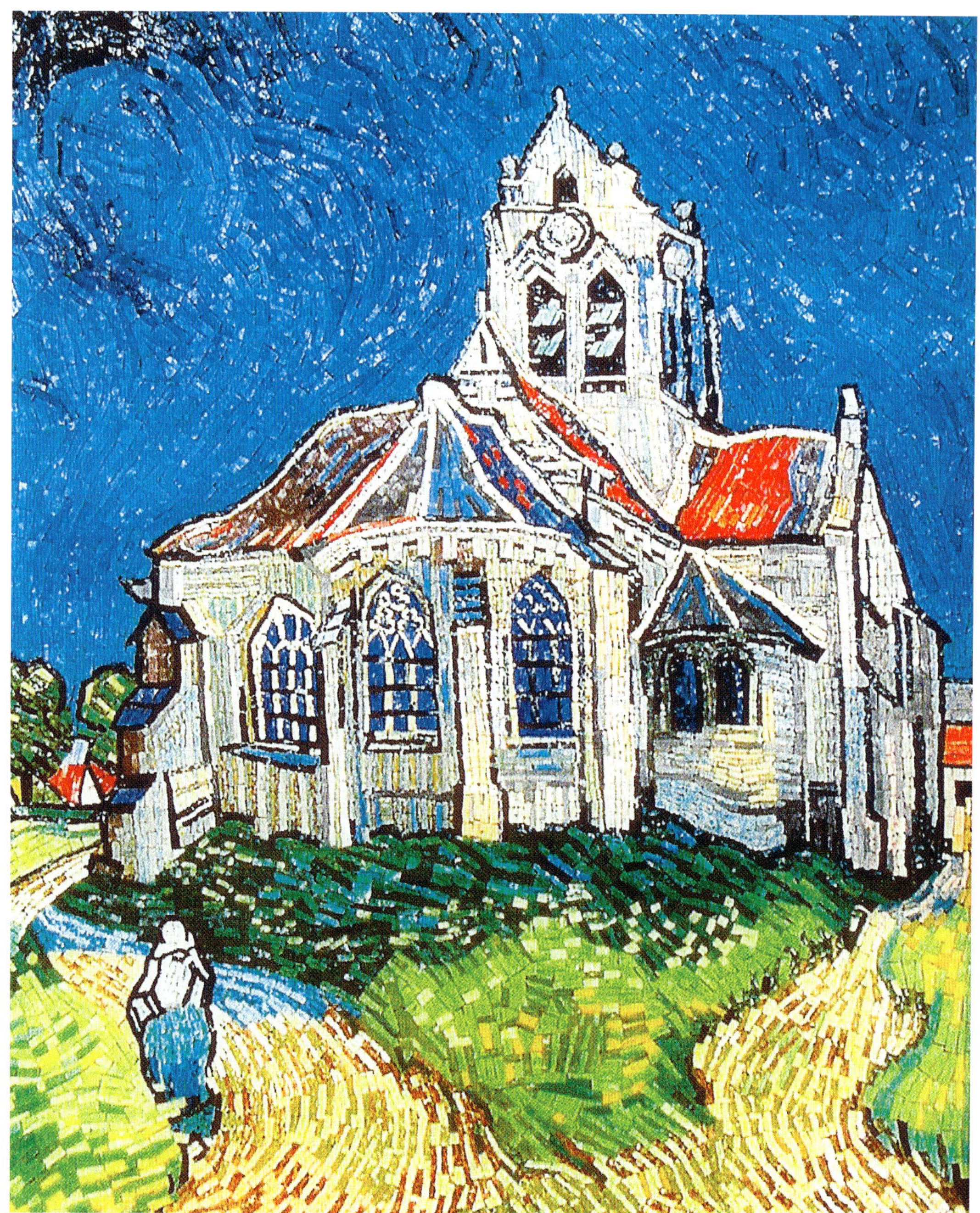

CHURCH OF AUVERS

cm. 60x75.

Cut and filament enamel technique, fixed with oily stucco onto an iron support tray.

Reproduction from the painting by Vincent Van Gogh, 1890;

Orsay Museum collection, Paris.

Courtesy of Dr. Richard Kent.

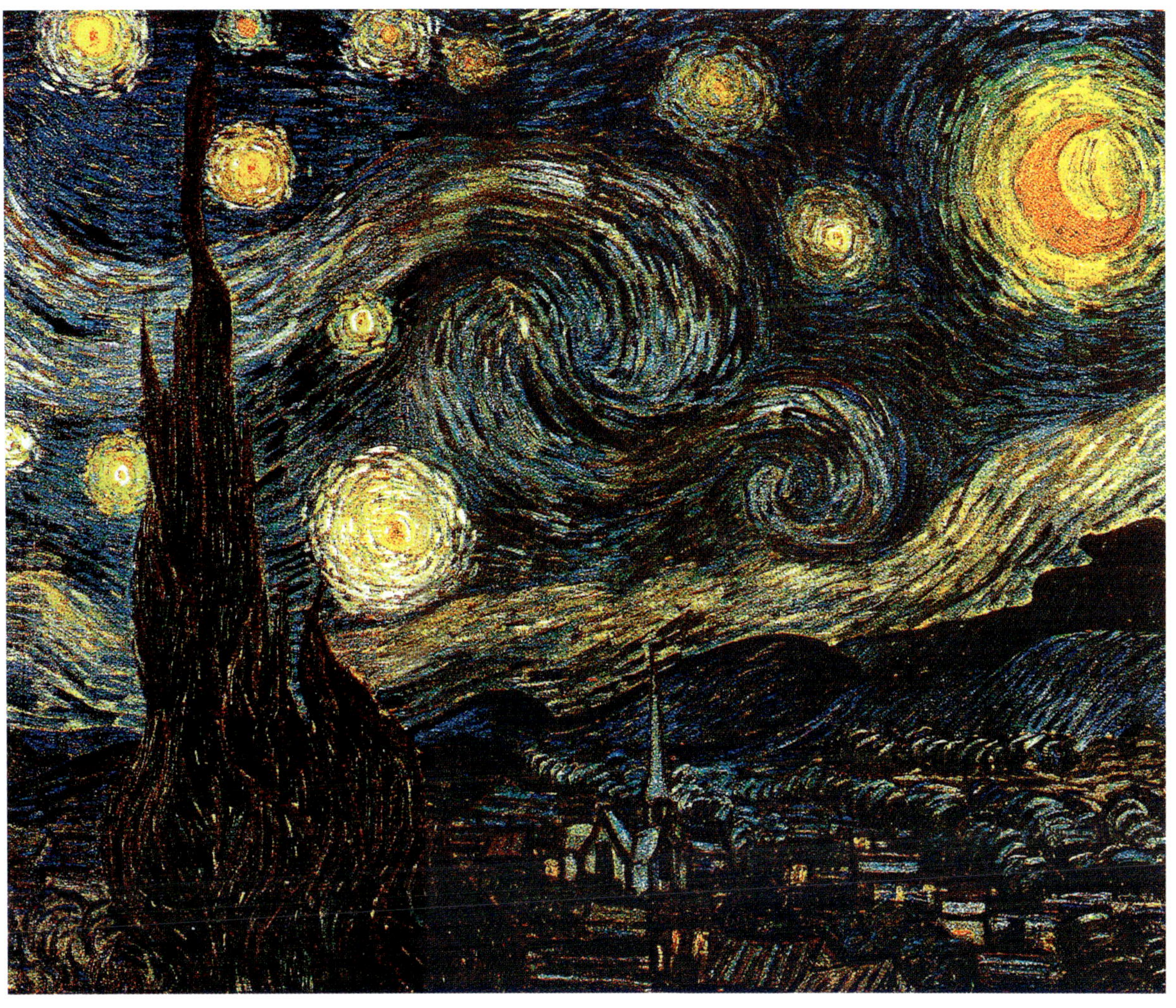

STARRY NIGHT

cm. 92x72.
Cut and filament enamel technique,
fixed with oily stucco onto an iron support tray.
Reproduction from the painting by Vincent Van Gogh, 1889;
MOMA collection, New York.
Courtesy of Mr. and Mrs. Ron Perey.

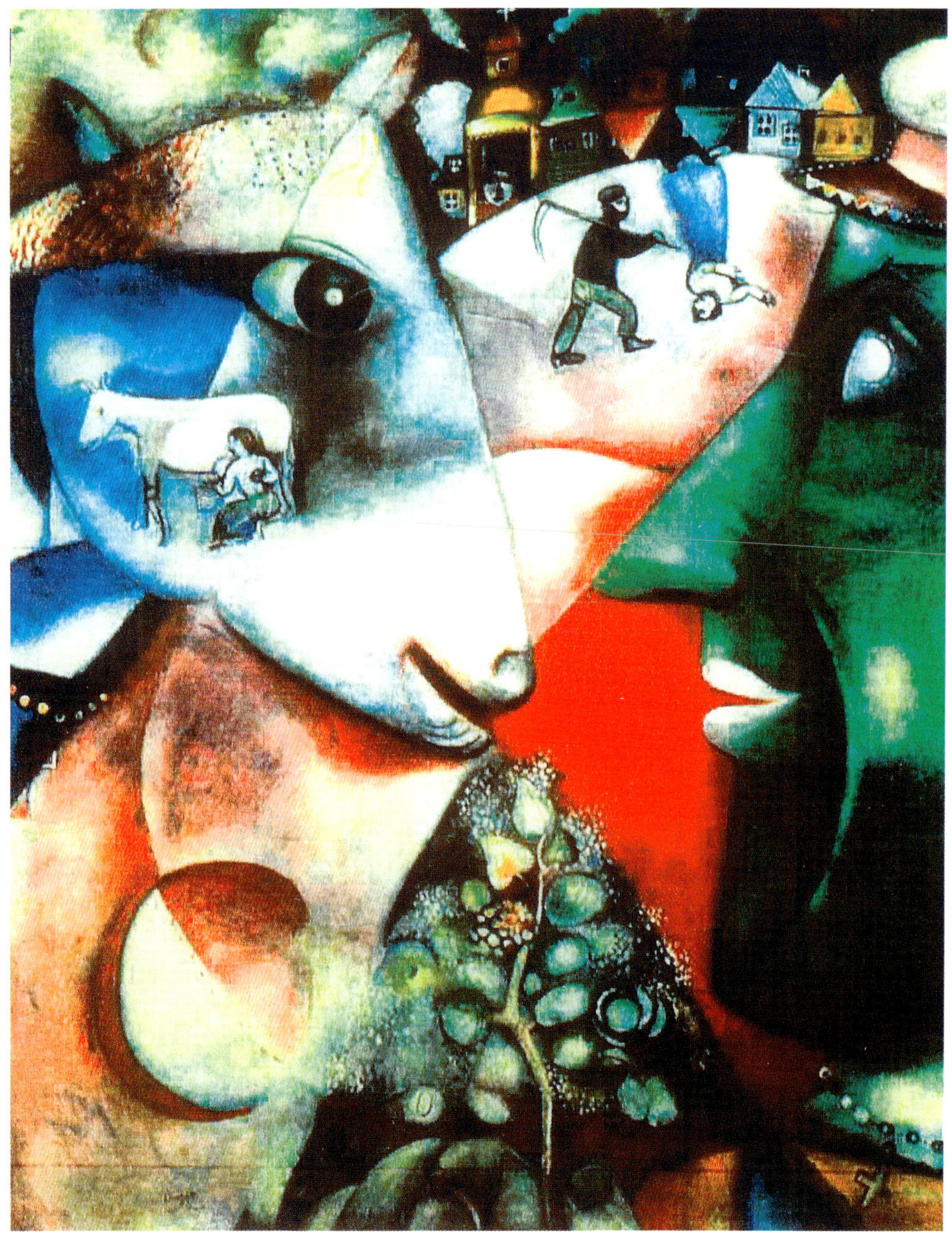

I AND THE VILLAGE

cm 80x100.
Cut and filament enamel technique,
fixed with oily stucco onto an iron support tray.
Reproduction from the painting by Marc Chagall, 1911;
MOMA collection, New York.
Courtesy of Mr. Steven Mihaylo.

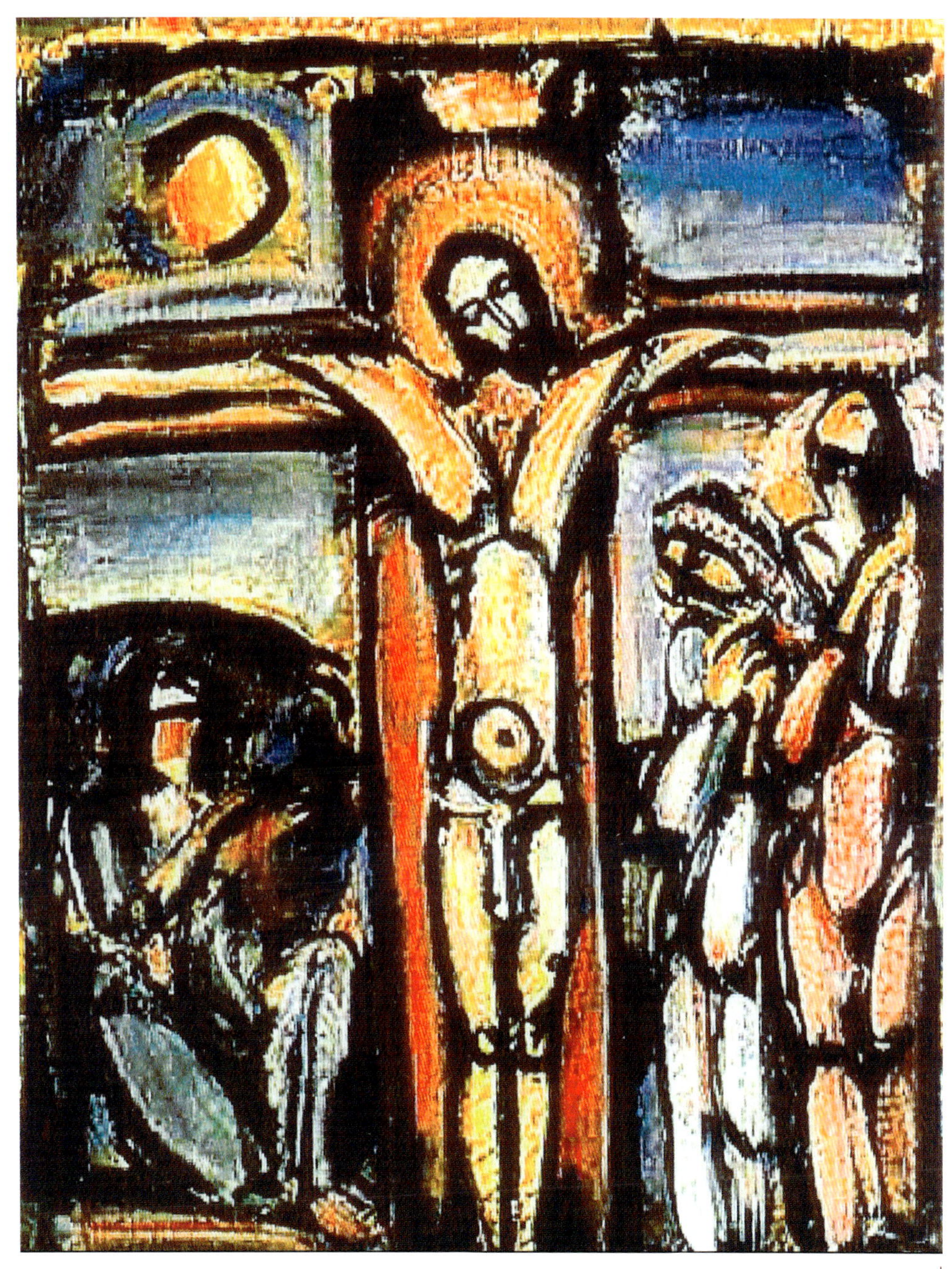

CRUCIFIXION

cm. 40x55.
Cut and filament enamel technique,
fixed with oily stucco onto an iron support tray.
Reproduction from the painting by Georges Rouault, 1939;
private collection of Rouault's family, Paris.
Courtesy of Mr. Gerald Rauenhorst.

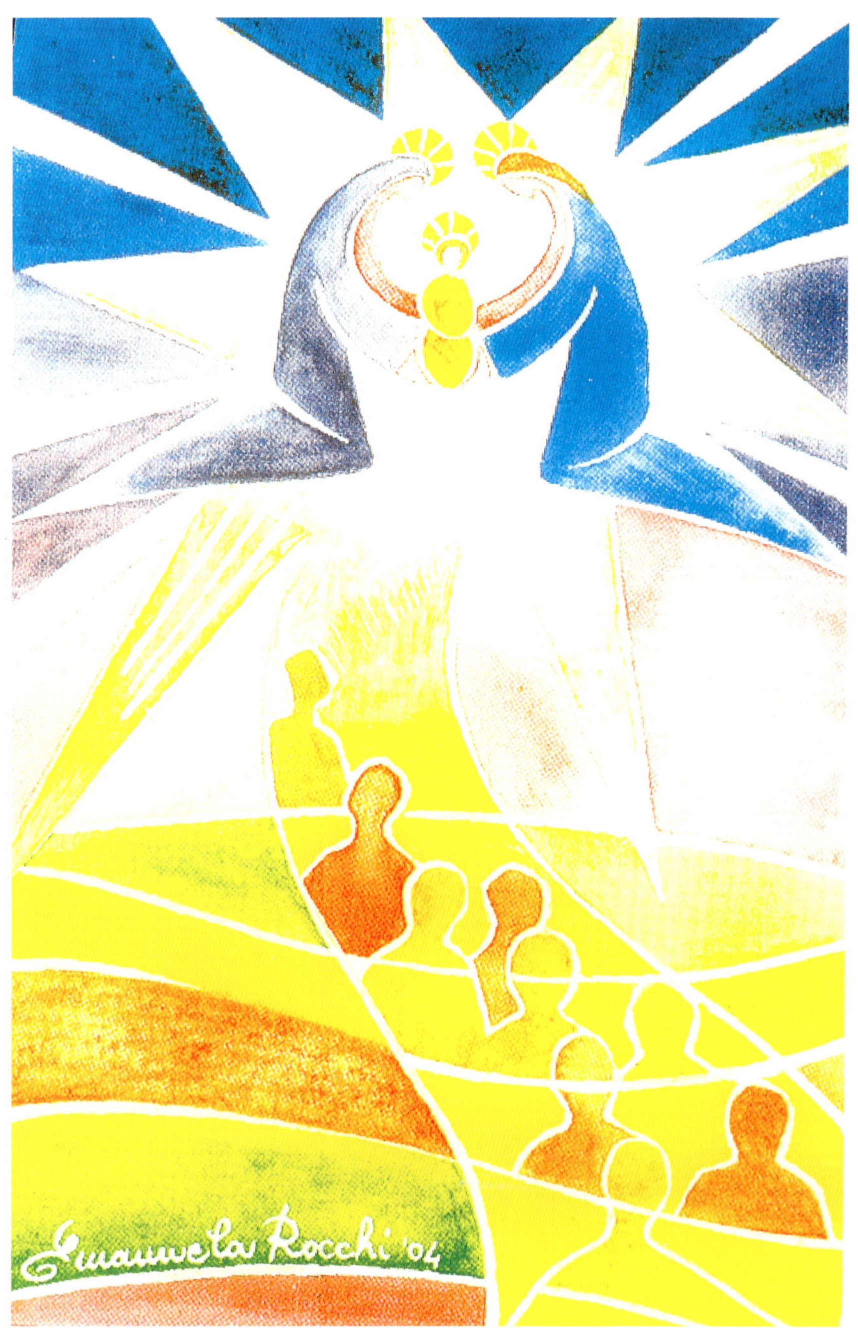

NATIVITY

cm. 40x60.
Cut and filament enamel technique,
fixed with oily stucco onto an iron support tray.
Original composition designed by Emanuela Rocchi,
mosaic artist of the Vatican Mosaic Studio, 2005.

Conclusion:

Reflections by the Vatican Mosaic Studio staff Craftsmen and Craftswomen

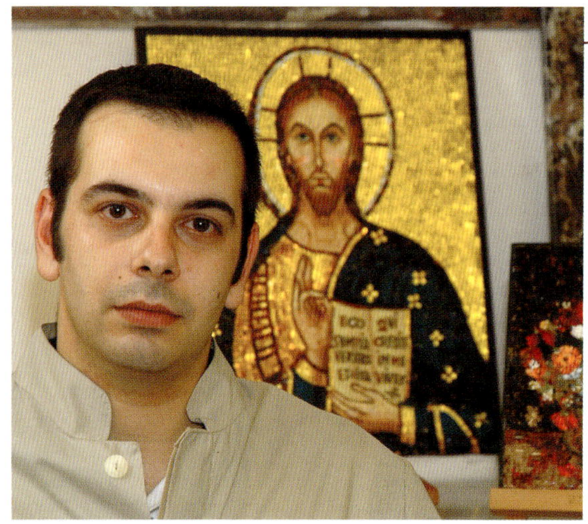

Alessandro Guisti

Our eyes love to see that which is beautiful. Our spirit is delighted and gladdened when the beauty of creation comes to be represented, with a chromatism of colors, through a work of art such as a mosaic. I am grateful to God that he has returned to me a humble way to express my artistic sensibilities at this exhibit of the Vatican Mosaic Studio.

Valentino Buonaguro

One asks oneself about the motive that, at the end of ancient times, pushed many artists to have a preference for the mosaic as compared to other decorative forms. The most logical response is that they wanted to make their own art to last as long as possible. The artists chose from all the techniques that one which had always given the impression of the greatest stability.

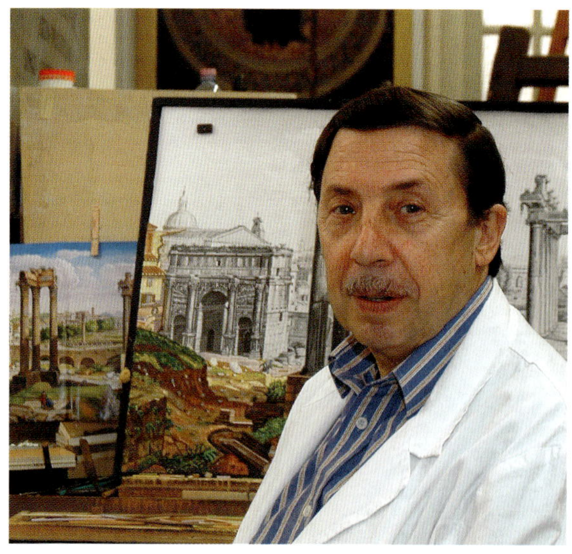

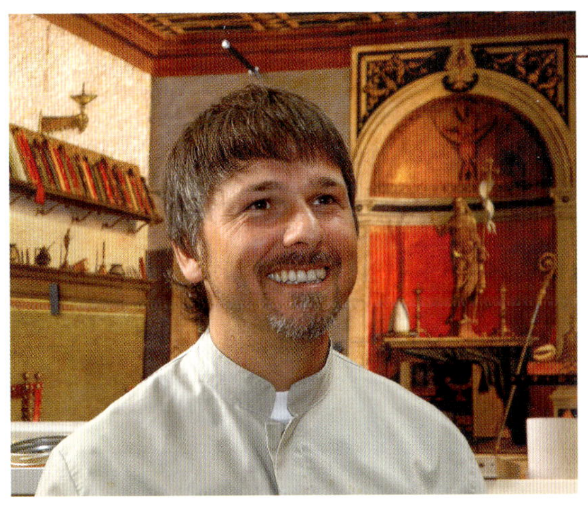

Cesare Bella

A great mosaicist, Michelangelo Barberi, active in the middle of the nineteenth century, invited aspiring mosaicists to embrace mosaic art "artistically and philosophically". The mosaicist is not in fact simply a craftsman but an "author" in the fullest sense of the word. The formless material comes from his shaping, developing in its own nature and transforming the mosaic so that to the layman it would seem to be a simple puzzle to be put together but that is the reality of the art, the fruit of his tactile, visual, pictorial sensibility; a sensibility that the true mosaicist possesses like an innate talent.

The enthusiasm, the passion, and the profound awareness to continue an illustrious, noble, and ancient tradition with humility and pride live in him.

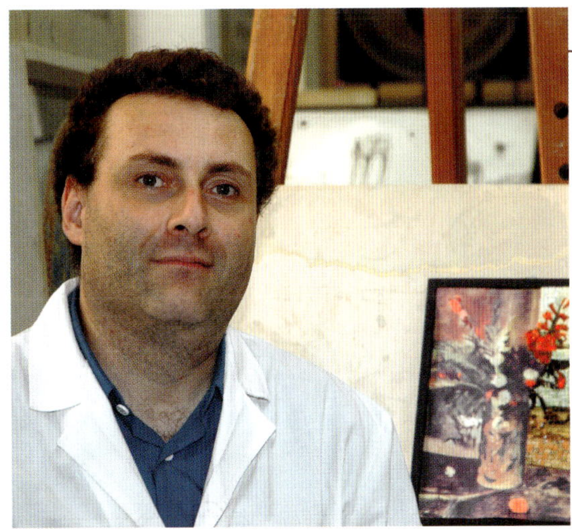

Adriano Galise

The mosaicist has almost always occupied a secondary place in the history of art, because he was limited to copying, for example, pictorial subjects. But for me the most fascinating manifestation of art is when one synthesizes complicated pictorial expressions and gives a certain luminosity that can be defined as eternal.

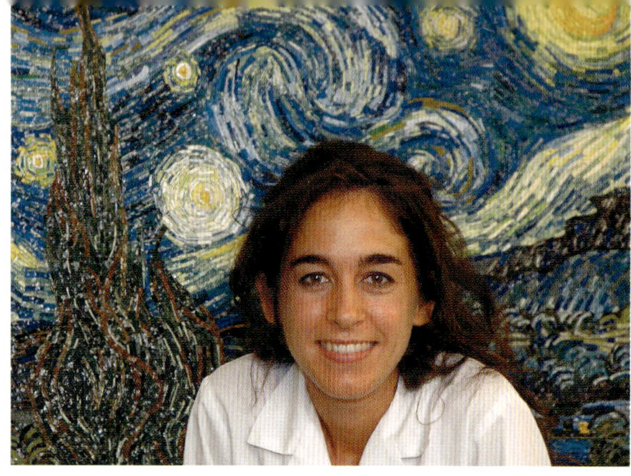

Emanuela Rocchi

It is an honor and a great satisfaction for me to be part of the Vatican Mosaic Studio team. That which renders this work very fascinating is the awareness of being the continuation of a school that has lasted for centuries and the possibility of apprehending day after day a refined and sophisticated technique. To be surrounded by an infinite number of colors, to mold and give form to the tesserae, and to weave and match one to the other, bringing them together, is to harness life to the picture.

Nicoletta Marino

The union of art and artisanship arrives as a flash of eternity on the terrestrial world.

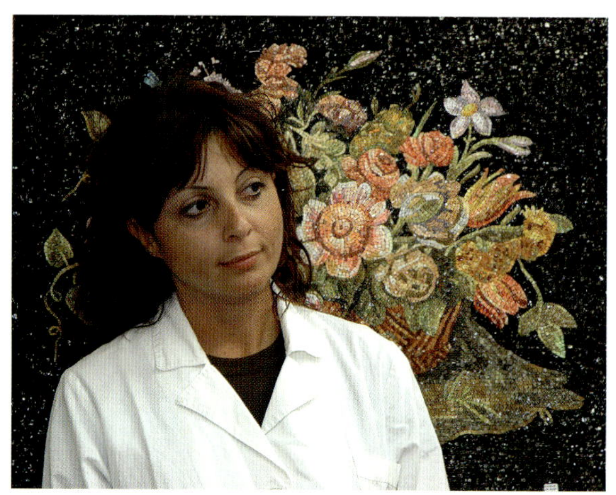

Carla Pirolli

The Mosaic Studio boasts a centuries-old tradition, recognized throughout the whole world; it has been for me an honor to be part of this team that has seen the birth of great masters. I find it truly edifying to work at the realization of mosaic compositions, to create diverse color tones, to give luminosity with gradations of diverse colors, to interpret that which the painters wished to transmit to us, and to observe as infinite, tesserae that would be able to resemble brushstroke.

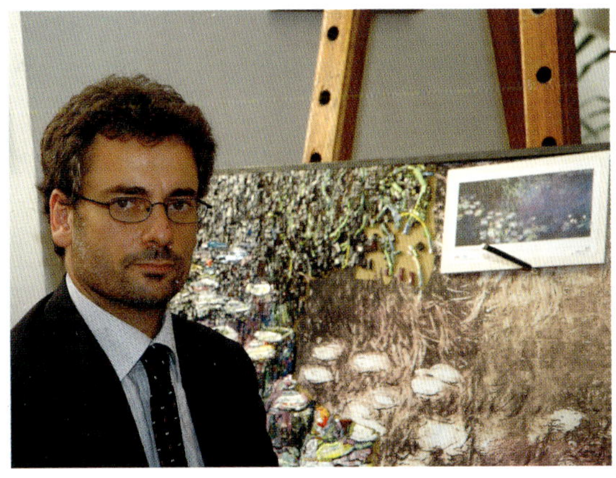

Paolo Di Buono

To work for the Vatican Mosaic Studio signifies being able to be a part of, despite ourselves, a history much greater than ourselves. The unique artistic experience, in fact connects one to many generations of mosaicists who slowly and forcefully, in the course of centuries, worked to decorate and to embellish the Basilica constructed on the Tomb of the Apostle Peter. For us, the weight, the responsibility, but also the joy of conserving and caring for it, as it is realized, comes from the practice of this art with one eye to the tradition and one to tomorrow.

Gabriele Mattiacci

The colors of nature are one of the things with which I have always been fascinated. Today I can say that the Mosaic Studio offers me the possibility to synthesize in a work of art the innumerable tones of colors and light that we observe in the world today. To see the idea emerge from a preliminary drawing, tessera after tessera, one time of a man or a ruin in the landscape, and to place the ultimate tessera to compete the work of art, are always a cause of emotion for me. I believe that my greatest satisfaction would come from the

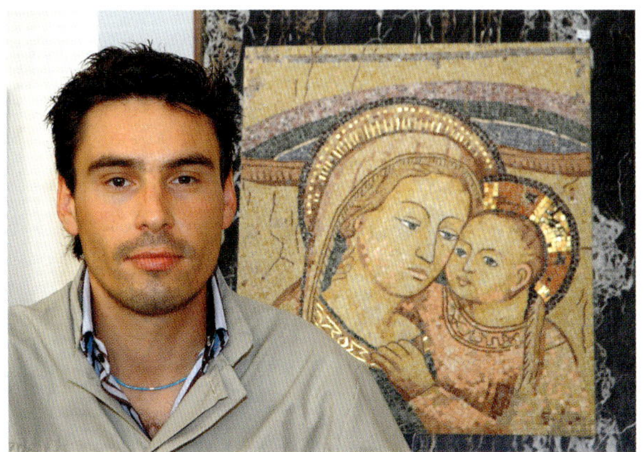

recognition that in a particular mosaic there is a paternity that it renders unique and unrepeatable because the form of the tesserae cannot be copied exactly. I like to be a part of the grand emotion that takes in hand one portion of mosaics finished in centuries past by great workers and then restoring it, and also the awareness that after however many months, millions of people will admire the mosaic in its original splendor. This happened to me in the restoration of one of the cupolas of St. Peter's Basilica. Three years or so ago, I was no less amazed by entering the gallery of the Studio and realizing the responsibility of learning and handing down with passion and competence the antique mosaic art.

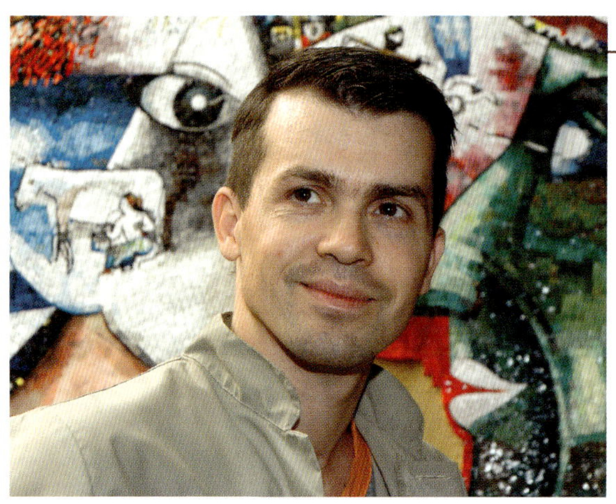

Claudiu Ungureanu

The end of art is to transmit a sentiment through knowledge of the truth, by seeking for it with happiness. The language of the mosaic coincides with the language of painting, of music, and of poetry. The only difference is the technique.

WE ARE MOST GRATEFUL FOR THE FOLLOWING WHO HAVE MADE THIS EXHIBITION POSSIBLE

The Fabbrica di San Pietro:
- His Eminence Francesco Cardinal Marchisano, Archpriest of St. Peter's Basilica
- His Excellency Archbishop Angelo Comastri, President of the Fabbrica
- Dr. Cristina Carlo-Stella, Chief of Staff of the Fabbrica.

The Catholic Cultural Heritage Center:
- Excellency Archbishop Alfred C. Hughes, Archbishop of New Orleans
- Reverend Monsignor Crosby W. Kern, Director
- Dr. Charles Nolan, Archivist,
- Archdiocese of New Orleans
- Mrs. Barbara Turner Windhorst, Chair of the Board
- Mrs. Phyllis Taylor, Exhibition Chair

The State of Louisiana:
- Hon. Kathleen Babineaux Blanco, Governor
- Hon. Mitch Landrieu, Lt. Governor
- Hon. John A. Alario, Jr., State Representative
- Hon. Francis Heitmeier, State Senator
- Hon. Juan A. LaFonta, State Representative.

Art Sponsors:
- Mr. Marshall Miller
- Mr. & Mrs. Wayne Huizenga
- Mr. & Mrs. Thomas Monaghan
- Mr. Charles Mires
- Mr. Eugenio Galindo
- Ms. Julie Mills
- Mr. and Mrs. David Collis
- Dr. and Mrs. Harley Stock
- Ms. Peggy Schulze
- Dr. Richard Kent, MD
- Mr. and Mrs. Ron Perey
- Mr. Gerald Rauenhorst
- Mr. Steven Mihaylo

Patrons:
- Mr. Joseph Canizaro
- Mrs. Phyllis Taylor
- Mr. Ira J. Middleberg

Planning Committee:
- Rev. Msgr. Crosby W. Kern
- Deacon Richard Brady
- Dr. Charles Nolan
- Ms. Bonnie Hymel Trentacoste
- Mr. Richard Treuting
- Mrs. Barbara Turner Windhorst

In Kind Contributors:

Louisiana State Dept. of Tourism
Louisiana State Museum
The City of New Orleans
The Historic New Orleans Collection
The New Orleans Museum of Art
The New Orleans Center For the Arts
GrayLine of New Orleans
The Hotel Monteleone

The Publishers regret any sponsor omissions due to publication deadlines.

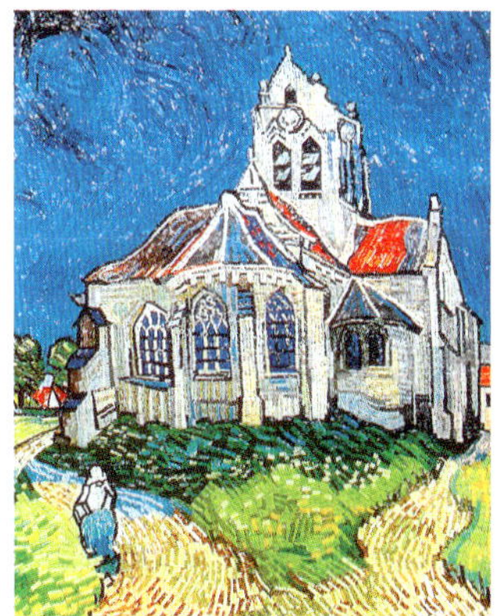

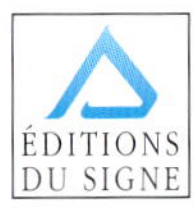

PUBLISHER:
Éditions du Signe
B.P. 94 - 67038 Strasbourg - France
Tel: (0033) (0) 3 88 78 91 91
Fax: (0033) (0) 3 88 78 91 99
Email: info@editionsdusigne.fr
www.editionsdusigne.fr

PUBLISHING DIRECTOR: Christian Riehl

DIRECTOR OF PUBLICATION: Joëlle Bernard

Text and photos: Vatican Mosaic Exhibition
Catholic Cultural Heritage Center
Old Ursuline Convent
Archdiocese of New Orleans

Design and Layout: Juliette Roussel

Photoengraving: Atelier du Signe (106882)

ISBN 13: 978-2-7468-1741-8
ISBN 10: 2-7468-1741-1

Printed in Spain by G. HARRIS